AF327195

CHILDHOODS PAST

Children's art of the twentieth century

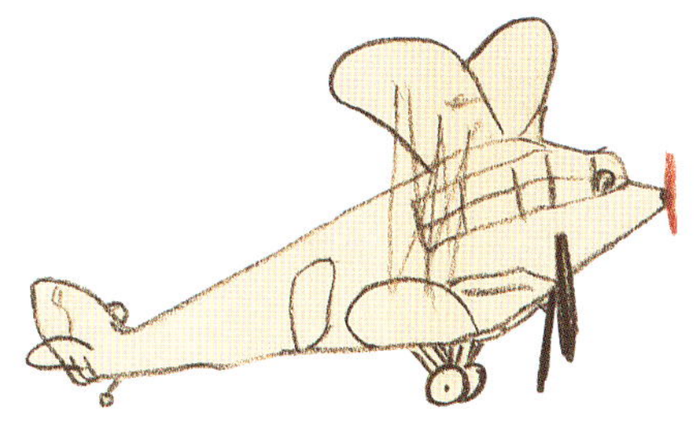

■ national gallery of **australia**

© National Gallery of Australia, Canberra, ACT, 1999.
All rights reserved. No part of this publication may be
reproduced or transmitted in any form or by any means,
electronic or mechanical, including photocopy, recording
or any information storage and retrieval system without
permission in writing from the publisher.

Produced by the Publications Department of the
National Gallery of Australia, Canberra
Designer: Kirsty Morrison
Editor: Karen Leary
Printed by NCP, Canberra

The National Gallery of Australia gratefully acknowledges
the generous assistance of the Gordon Darling Foundation
in the publication of this book.

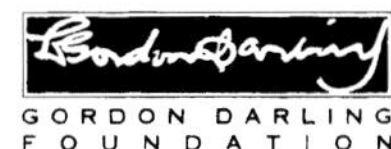

Cataloguing-in-Publication data
Childhoods past: children's art of the twentieth century

Bibliography

ISBN 0 642 54134 5

1. Derham, Frances - Art collections - Exhibitions. 2. Frances
Derham Collection - Exhibitions. 3. National Gallery of
Australia - Exhibitions. 4. Children's art - Australia -
Exhibitions. 5. Children's art - Private collections - Australian
Capital Territory - Canberra - Exhibitions. 6. Children's art -
Australian Capital Territory - Canberra. 7. Art, Modern - 20th
century - Australia - Exhibitions. I. Piscitelli, Barbara.
II. White, Margaret, A. H. III Title.

704.0544

Distributed in Australia by:
Thames and Hudson
11 Central Boulevard Business Park, Port Melbourne, Victoria
3207

Distributed in the United Kingdom by:
Thames and Hudson
30–34 Bloomsbury Street, London WC1B 3QP

Distributed in the United States of America by:
University of Washington Press
1326 Fifth Avenue, Ste. 555, Seattle, WA 98101-2604

(cover) **Unknown** Vienna *Animal, person, house* c.1930 (detail)
Frances Derham Collection, National Gallery of Australia

This publication accompanies the National Gallery
of Australia's travelling exhibition *Childhoods Past: Children's
art of the twentieth century*, organised in collaboration with the
Queensland Institute of Technology and Macquarie University
and shown at:
Customs House Gallery, Brisbane Qld
10 September – 10 October 1999

Rockhampton Regional Gallery, Rockhampton Qld
31 January – 27 February 2000

Macquarie University, Sydney NSW
13 March – 12 May 2000

Old Treasury Building, Melbourne Vic
8 June – 30 July 2000

New Land Gallery, Port Adelaide SA
18 August – 24 September 2000

Geraldton Regional Art Gallery, Geraldton WA
7 October – 26 November 2000

Wagga Wagga Regional Art Gallery, Wagga Wagga NSW
9 February – 25 March 2001

National Gallery of Australia, Canberra ACT
31 March – 9 July 2001

The tour of this exhibition is made possible by

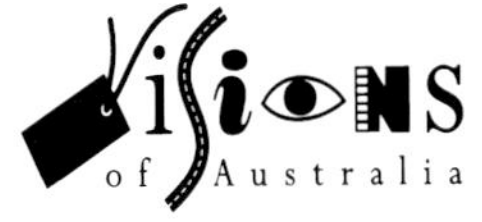

Visions of Australia is the Commonwealth's national touring
exhibitions grant program. It assists with the development or
touring of cultural exhibitions across Australia.

CONTENTS

FROM THE MINISTER

The National Gallery of Australia, in partnership with Queensland University
of Technology and Macquarie University, has drawn upon the impressive collection
of children's paintings and drawings collected by Frances Derham from the 1930s to the
1970s to present this memorable exhibition.

This touring exhibition is a rare insight into the creative spirit of children aged five
to fourteen. The 80 children's works are personal depictions of life's experiences
— such as the 1956 Melbourne Olympics, the Queen visiting Australia, mustering
cattle in remote areas, school life and playing in the snow.

The expressive nature of children's art and how they reveal their view on the world
is an important part of our cultural heritage.

The catalogue, generously funded by the Gordon Darling Foundation, will be
an invaluable and timely addition to the ongoing research into the history of art
education this century.

Childhoods Past: Children's art of the twentieth century will be seen by many communities
throughout its national tour and will encourage both parents and children to explore
their artistic creativity.

The Hon. Peter McGauran MP
Minister for the Arts and the Centenary of Federation

FROM THE DIRECTOR

Childhoods Past: Children's art of the twentieth century is the result of an important collaboration between Queensland University of Technology, Macquarie University and the National Gallery of Australia. The exhibition is derived from the Frances Derham Collection which was donated to the Gallery in 1976. It is a collection of great integrity and the result of a lifetime's endeavour and commitment.

We pay tribute to Frances Derham and are delighted to offer the Australian public the opportunity to view *Childhoods Past* by making these works available to audiences in regional and metropolitan centres across the country.

At the cusp of a new millennium, this exhibition celebrates the genius and creativity of children all around the world. This insightful exhibition is a *must see,* not only for those who enjoy the refreshing and innocent works of children but also those who may recall their own attempts at grasping visual expression, or who are aware of the influences of children's art upon many major artists of the twentieth century.

I would like to congratulate the participating venues for their support and commitment to an exhibition that is both educational and inspirational. We gratefully acknowledge Visions of Australia, who have made the development and tour of this exhibition possible, the Gordon Darling Foundation for support of the catalogue published in association with the exhibition, and Australian Air Express, an ongoing and loyal supporter of the National Gallery's Travelling Exhibitions Program.

Dr Brian Kennedy, Director
National Gallery of Australia

FOREWORD

Queensland University of Technology (QUT) is pleased to be a partner in this collaborative exhibition, *Childhoods Past: Children's art of the twentieth century*, which builds upon the current breadth of research and practice undertaken within the University. This exhibition has seen the realisation of ten years of research on Frances Derham by Barbara Piscitelli, Senior Lecturer, QUT. Her expertise and knowledge of the collection has proved invaluable to the partnership.

It is an important time for reflection on the past and planning for the future. The paintings and drawings in *Childhoods Past* highlight social and political issues, cultural traditions and the significance of these events in the minds of children. The images within the exhibition will undoubtedly spark renewed interest in children and their art.

The launch of *Childhoods Past* coincides with the 30th World Congress of the International Society for Education through Art, (InSEA) held in September 1999 in Brisbane, and provides an ideal opportunity to acknowledge the contribution which Frances Derham made to InSEA over many years.

In cooperation with our partners, we are proud to bring this exhibition to a large number of Australians, thus assuring widespread diffusion of a rich cultural and educational message.

Professor R.D. Gibson
Vice-Chancellor
Queensland University of Technology

FOREWORD

Macquarie University supports the development of a wide range of exhibitions through its museums and collections and is proud to be involved with *Childhoods Past: Children's art of the twentieth century*. We are delighted to support an exhibition that further disseminates the work of Frances Derham and highlights the importance of this nationally and internationally significant collection, which is part of the collection of the National Gallery of Australia. Margaret White of the Institute of Early Childhood, Macquarie University, worked with Frances Derham when she was a student in Melbourne and has been a valuable contributor in the area of social, cultural and artistic influences on children's art in the twentieth century.

Childhoods Past focuses on children's art making, through images that present the richness of children's representations of their world. This exhibition has the potential to influence ways in which children's art is viewed in our society and to promote understanding about the significance of the visual arts in the lives of children.

Macquarie University is delighted to be hosting *Childhoods Past* at the new Macquarie University Gallery in Sydney as part of the national tour.

Professor Di Yerbury AM
Vice-Chancellor
Macquarie University

INTRODUCTION

A gift to the nation:
The Frances Derham Collection
in the National Gallery of Australia

The collection is an extraordinary one which in its completeness is certainly without parallel in any art gallery anywhere.[1]

So wrote James Mollison, Director of the National Gallery of Australia to Frances Derham in 1976, six years before the Gallery opened. Mollison was referring to Derham's vast collection of child art, some 10,000 works, which she intended to give to the Gallery.

The collection was the visual evidence of Derham's life's work and influence as a pre-eminent child art educator. She saw children's works as artistic treasures and through her tireless endeavours was a major influence in the changing attitudes to art education — from a rigorous and structured approach to one that celebrated freedom of artistic expression. In fact she has been called 'the mother of child art' in Australia.

The exhibition *Childhoods Past: Children's art of the twentieth century* is a celebration of the work of Frances Derham and of the children whose art she collected. Developed to provide a reflective view on the position of children and their art this century, it is divided into three themes: social and political events, personal and cultural identity, and school and family life. The images offer some extraordinary and unique historical moments and personal responses captured through the eyes of children.

Frances Derham had a strong desire to have her life's work placed somewhere safe for posterity and kept as a work in progress for future reference and research. To this end, between 1975 and her death in 1987, she wrote hundreds of letters to the National Gallery. These, along with the many other documents, records and correspondence now in the Gallery's archive, provide insight into the intensity of Derham's own research and her extraordinary gift to the nation.

On 19 February 1976, James Mollison visited Derham at her home in the Melbourne suburb of Kew and saw the quality of the collection. He said:

As a research tool in the education section it would be invaluable … I have no hesitation in recommending the acceptance of the gift of this material.[2]

Mollison instructed staff to arrange for the packing of the first instalment and wrote a submission to the Australian National Gallery (ANG) Interim Council. On 9 March 1976 the Council agreed to accept Frances Derham's gift.

For the next two years Mollison would receive at least one letter per month from Derham. In these she included references to her own work and that of other artists of her generation, reminiscences of working with children, invitations to dinner and exhibition openings and even a suggestion of who should run the new Gallery's education centre. Derham's energy was staggering and for Mollison, who had the responsibility of opening the country's most significant art gallery, his support for the project was admirable — his commitment possibly strengthened through years of being an art educator in Melbourne.

Derham was very keen for the Gallery to exhibit the works as soon as possible; Mollison was also looking forward to making the collection accessible to the Australian public. In 1979, the Year of the Child, a selection of works was exhibited in Adelaide, the National Gallery of Victoria and the David Jones Gallery, Sydney. This selection was subsequently exhibited at the Association for Modern Education School in Canberra in 1980.

During the intervening years several staff at the National Gallery became involved in the transfer of the collection from Derham's house in Melbourne to Canberra. In late 1980, Terence Measham was recruited from the Tate Gallery, London, to head the Education Centre at the Gallery. After arriving in Australia one of his first trips was to visit Derham. Measham was particularly keen to receive a group of works called 'Reach for the Apple', based on the theories of Viktor Lowenfeld, a leader in the field of art education.

In 1982 Jennifer Hoff joined the education staff at the Gallery and became the curator of the Frances Derham Collection. Hoff visited Derham in August 1982 and, with a research background in tribal art as well as education, she immediately focused on the work from Hermannsburg in Central Australia, Aurukun in North Queensland and New Britain, in Papua New Guinea.

With the official opening of the National Gallery in October 1982, the education staff's attention was centred on the 11,500 schoolchildren who visited in the first six weeks. However by early 1983 Hoff had returned to documenting the collection as she was concerned about the increasing frailty of Derham who was now nearing 88 years of age.

In April 1984 Hoff produced the most significant exhibition of work from the Frances Derham Collection thus far. Entitled *Drawings and paintings by children from Hermannsburg, Aurukun and Malabunga*, the exhibition, displayed at the National Gallery, focused on indigenous work from Northern Territory, Queensland and New Guinea. Well received, the display coincided with a conference at the Gallery, held by the Australian Institute of Aboriginal Studies, and was supported by a room brochure. This was to be the first of a series of exhibitions from the Derham collection which sadly did not eventuate.

In January 1986 Derham wrote:

The Child Art Collection is at last being finalised and I will notify when the last (work) goes in. I am now 91 as I think I told you and am largely confined to my bed ...[3]

Her last correspondence, dated 24 June 1987, focused on her life's commitment and work:

I do not know whether you have looked through what I have sent, which must be 10,000 now, or simply leave it to interested people or students who may ask to do so. I know that you will get someone on request next year and presumably putting it, minus the last four important boxes, on the computer ... I have myself, had the contents of these last boxes pretty well assessed and though the collections are varied, there is a typed account of contents in each.[4]

Frances Derham died a few months later, aged 92.

Early in 1988 the Gallery was approached by a prospective PhD student wishing to research the life and collections of Frances Derham. This was an exciting opportunity which would fulfil the original intention of the gift and advance the scholarship and understanding of Derham's work. The research of Barbara Piscitelli (lecturer at Queensland University of Technology) and completion of her doctorate on Frances Derham further developed the interest in the collection and potential exhibitions.

In 1994 an approach was made to National Gallery director Betty Churcher to relocate the collection to Melbourne. Through the commitment and quick action of the 'guardian' of the collection, Barbara Brinton, Manager of Education, a tragedy was averted and the collection remained in Canberra. To make the works more accessible the collection was relocated within the Gallery from the off-site storage area that had been its home.

The following year Lucienne Fontannez curated the travelling exhibition *Then and Now* (coincidentally, a title Derham had used many years before). The exhibition focused on Aboriginal children's work and the important Aboriginal works from the Derham collection toured nationally. Still a comprehensive exhibition of the collection had not been organised.

In 1996 Margaret White, a lecturer from Macquarie University who had for some time had an interest in the collection, co-curated a children's art exhibition *Drawing on the Art of Children* which contained 22 works from the Frances Derham Collection. The exhibition was displayed at Macquarie University and toured, most importantly, to Preshil School, Melbourne, the school where Derham had taught and where her interests in child art started:

> *... my understanding of child art began through working at 'Preshil'... [where] in 1934 I allowed about fifty children to draw with charcoal, and paint with calcimine, on easels, without direction from me other than preliminary gathering when I drew from them remarks and accounts about what they had done since they saw me, and then invited them to paint anything that had been specially interesting or exciting. I collected their work for a whole year...*[5]

Following the success of the Macquarie University exhibition it seemed it was now time to mount a travelling exhibition that would display the full range of the Derham collection. The most constructive way to present the exhibition was for the National Gallery to collaborate with Barbara Piscitelli and Margaret White, two academics in the field of early childhood, so the selection of works would appeal to both a scholarly and general audience.

In support of such a collaborative exhibition director Dr Brian Kennedy wrote:

> *Twenty five years after their donation to the National Gallery of Australia, this tour will enable the majority of these works to be seen publicly for the first time. It is a collection of great integrity and the result of a lifetime's endeavour and commitment — we owe Frances Derham and the broader Australian public the opportunity to view* Childhoods Past: Children's art of the twentieth century.[6]

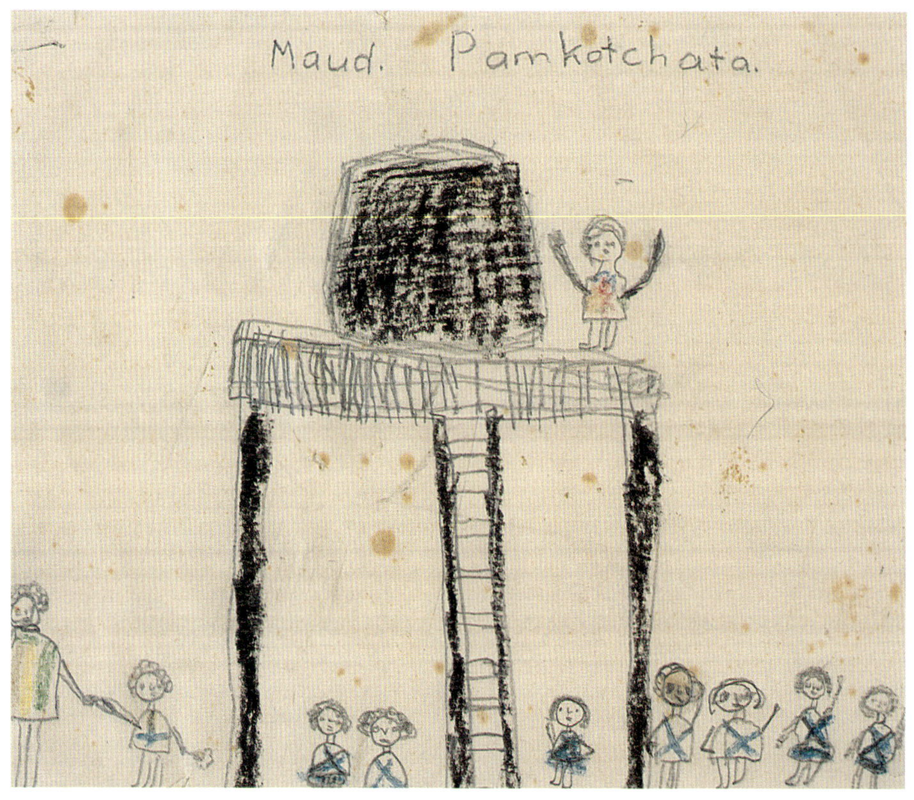

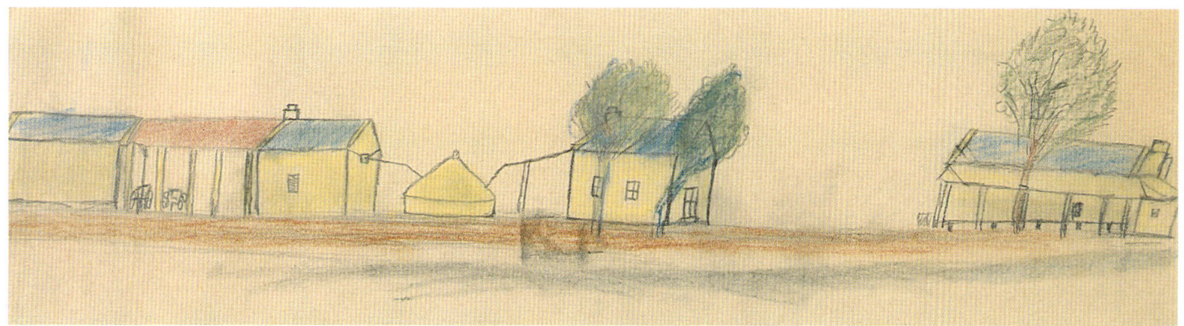

The Minister for the Arts, the Hon. Peter McGauran MP, visited the Gallery in May 1999 and saw the works proposed for the exhibition. Funding was then secured through the Federal Government's Visions of Australia program.

The history of the collection spreads throughout the twentieth century and its hidden power has drawn support from a broad range of committed individuals, most recently and importantly, the project officer for the exhibition, Barbara Poliness. To enable the exhibition to tour and to ensure the greatest number of people engage with the collection, an enormous amount of work has been provided by the staff of the National Gallery of Australia. Works have been photographed, published, scanned for the Internet, conserved, mounted, framed and packed to tour.

We are all under the same spell, the words ring out from the hundreds of letters, the thousands of words — staring out from the photos, would we dare let her down … as Derham wrote to Mollison in her second letter of 1975:

In the meantime, it is here for you to see…[7]

Ron Ramsey

1 James Mollison, Director, Australian National Gallery, note for file, 23 February 1976, held in National Gallery of Australia archives.
2 Ibid.
3 Frances Derham, letter to James Mollison, 22 January 1986, held in National Gallery of Australia archives.
4 Frances Derham, letter to James Mollison, 24 June 1987, held in National Gallery of Australia archives.
5 Frances Derham, letter to James Mollison, 20 February, 1976, held in National Gallery of Australia archives.
6 Dr Brian Kennedy, statement to Visions of Australia, January 1999.
7 Frances Derham, letter to James Mollison, 13 November 1975, held in National Gallery of Australia archives.

(above) **Immanuel** Australia, Hermannsburg *Homestead* 1938
(opposite) **Maud Pamkotchata** Australia, Aurukun *Mrs Derham on the water tank* 1948

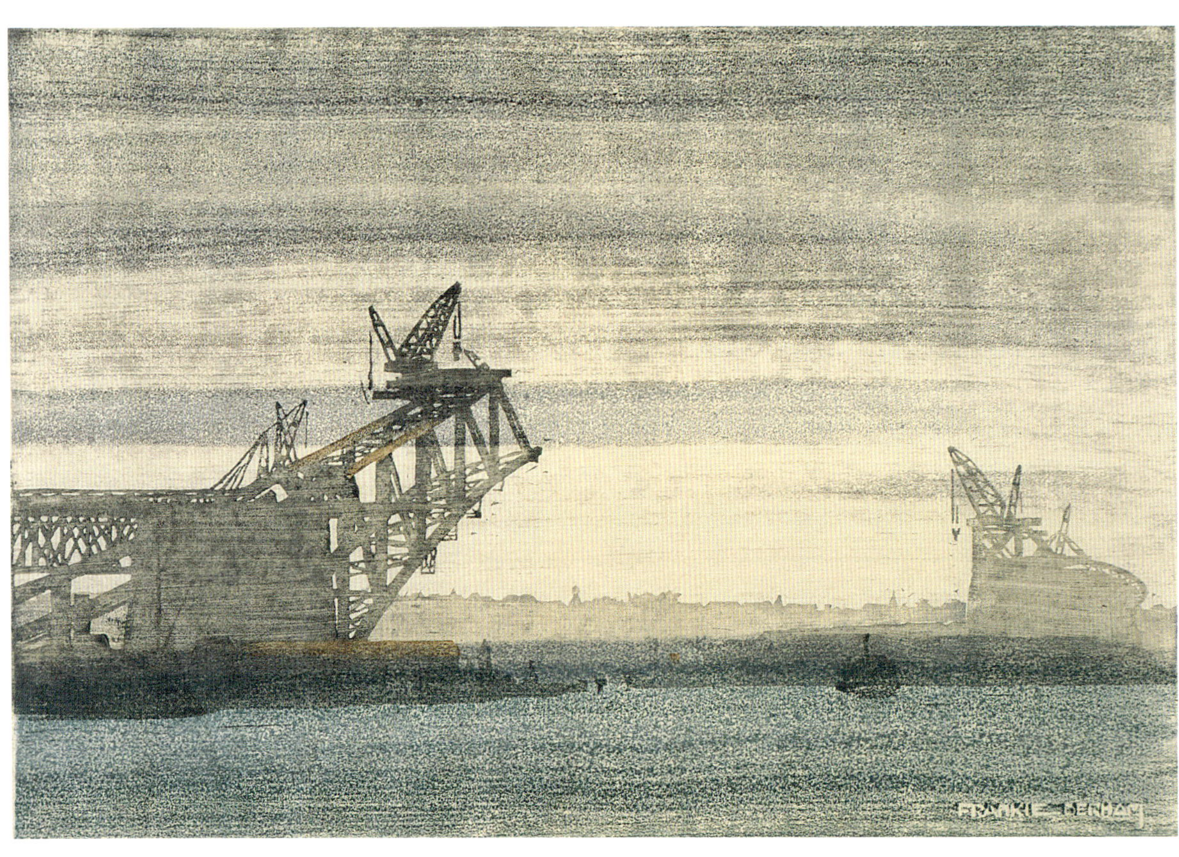

FRANKIE DENHAM

FRANCES DERHAM
Artist, teacher, collector

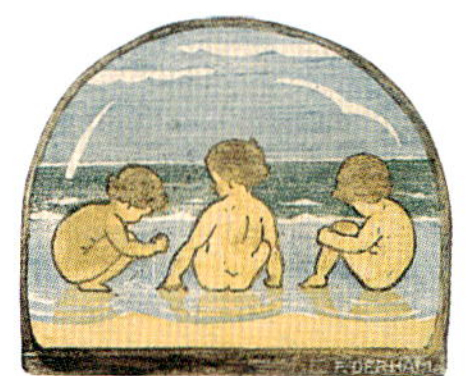

Frances Derham MBE was an educator and artist who, over more than half a century, collected children's art from Australia and throughout the world. A passionate advocate for children and their work, Derham played a pivotal role in shaping the direction of art education in Australia.

Derham, known as Frankie to family and friends, was born Frances Alexandra Mabel Letitia Anderson in Malvern, Victoria in 1894, the daughter of Irish immigrants who had come to Australia in search of work. Her early education was disrupted when the family moved, first to New Zealand, then England and Ireland, returning to Australia in 1907. The eldest daughter, Frankie helped her mother run the household, but also took special interest in working with her father, a consultant engineer, drafting drawings and blueprints.

Frankie's parents encouraged their daughter's rich imagination — while in New Zealand she began art classes at the local branch of the South Kensington Art School, and in Ireland attended the Royal School of Art for a time. By the age of 16, back in Australia, Frankie convinced her parents to send her to the National Gallery School. One of her instructors there was Frederick McCubbin. She later attended a full-time art teacher program at Swinburne Technical College and after graduating in 1916 took up a teaching position with the college.

In 1917 she married a doctor, Alfred Plumley Derham, who later assisted his wife in the manufacture of non-toxic paints for children. As married women were not permitted to teach, Derham left her position at the college and did not return to teaching for more than a decade. The couple had four children and during the 1920s, Derham's life revolved around family needs and taking an active role in numerous organisations, such as the Arts and Crafts Society of Victoria.

In 1929 the society invited her to give a lecture on Aboriginal art at the National Museum of Victoria during the first major exhibition of Aboriginal art held in a public gallery. This led Derham to correspond with anthropologist Charles P. Mountford and Rex Batterbee, the artist in residence at Hermannsburg Mission in central Australia. Her commitment to Aboriginal art and education became firmly set over the following years. In 1938 she visited Hermannsburg, then a decade later Aurukun in Queensland, to study the art of Aboriginal children.

(above) **Frances Derham** *Tom, David and Bill at the seaside* (c.1932–33)
National Gallery of Australia
(opposite) **Frances Derham** *Sydney bridge* 1929 National Gallery of Australia

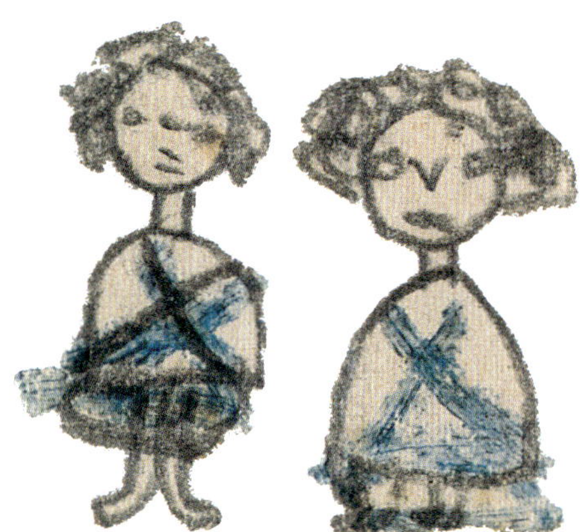

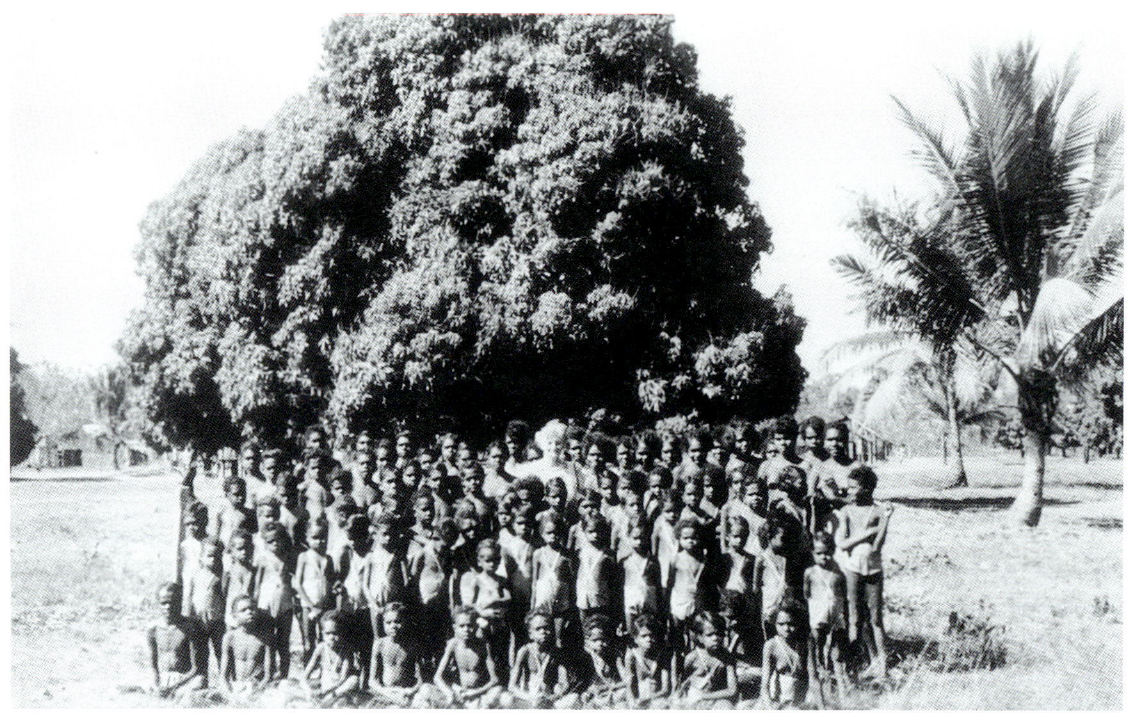

During the 1920s Derham's own work as an artist was relegated to the early hours of the morning or holidays, however she continued to practice and took lessons from Mary Cecil Allen in 1926 and Ethel Spowers in 1929. Derham continued to produce her own art throughout her life; her best-known works are her prints, several of which are held within the collections of the National Gallery of Australia and the National Gallery of Victoria.

Derham returned to teaching in 1929, working part-time at the Melbourne Kindergarten Training College, a position vacated by Ethel Spowers. She remained a lecturer with the college until 1964.

During the mid 1930s Derham underwent a major shift in her thinking on a number of areas. She had begun to espouse the cause of Modernism in art, thereby alienating herself from the mainstream of Australian art. She also began to align herself with progressive education. In 1937 she met Christine Heinig, an educator from the United States who helped Derham synthesise her ideas into a coherent framework for early childhood art education. Heinig was the new principal of the Melbourne Kindergarten Training College and brought with her considerable practical knowledge on the latest nursery school practices in the United States. She also brought an impressive touring exhibition of children's art from five continents which had been organised by the Progressive Education Association. Both the exhibition and Heinig's professional knowledge served as a catalyst for change. By 1939 Derham's syllabus in art for kindergarten teacher trainees had shifted from a teacher-centred focus to the more child-centred approach advocated by Heinig.

(above) Frances Derham with children at Aurukun, 1948 National Gallery of Australia Research Library

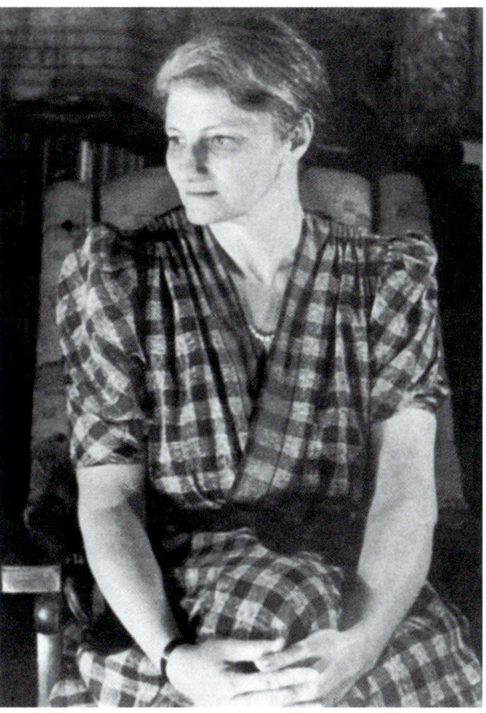

Art education for children in the early part of the century had been very structured and highly prescriptive, based on the principles of copying and following directions of the artist/teacher. Derham had at first taught strictly in this academic style, mirroring her own art training. However while teaching at the Kindergarten Training College, she began to change her approach. Around the same time she took a position teaching at Melbourne's progressive school, Preshil. Here, for the first time, her pupils were young children. In an effort to understand the children's art, and to build upon her own research into new techniques for teaching art, Derham began to collect drawings and paintings from Preshil. She was astonished at what they revealed about individual children and their artistic development.

From this time on, Derham advocated more freedom of expression in children's art and began to espouse the philosophies of Sir Herbert Read and Viktor Lowenfeld. As an art lecturer in various teacher training courses in Melbourne over the next three decades, Derham became a powerful force for change in art education practices. She recorded the fundamental elements of her views of teaching art in a best selling book *Art for the Child Under Seven*, first published in l961 and currently still in use as a reference in some early childhood teacher training programs.

Throughout her teaching career, Derham also maintained an active role with numerous organisations to advance changes in art education, including the influential Standing Committee for Art in Education at the University of Melbourne. Her daily diaries record a routine

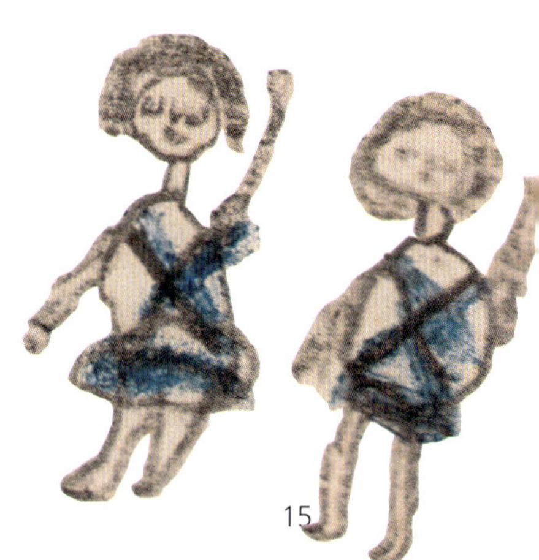

(above) Frances Derham, c.1940 Frances Derham Collection, the University of Melbourne Archives

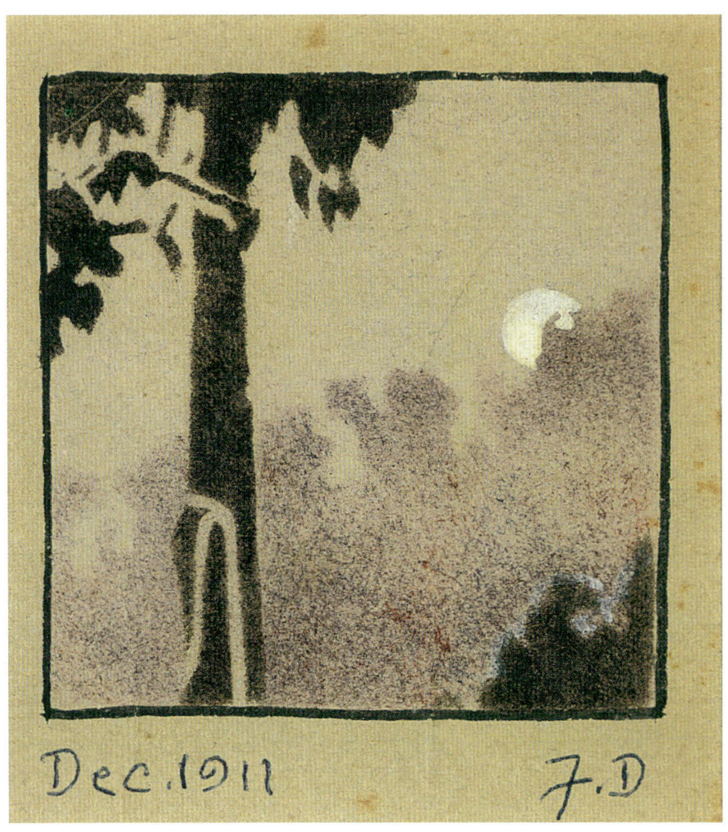

of meetings and events: as a student in the studio of George Bell, a Melbourne artist represented in the National Gallery's collection; as a lecturer at the Melbourne Kindergarten Training College; and as a member and leader of state, national and international associations. In 1950 Derham was awarded an MBE and many have assumed that her efforts in art education were the reason for this distinguished honour. However, this is not the case. Derham received her King's Birthday honour for her contribution to social welfare services, especially for her work in the AIF Women's Association and the Kew Community Aid Association during World War II.

In 1954, Derham became involved in a UNESCO sponsored seminar on art education held in Melbourne. At that meeting, she became aware of the International Society for Education through Art (InSEA), part of a worldwide movement to encourage cross-cultural understanding. In 1958, the Art Teachers Association of Victoria (ATAV) became a member of InSEA and Frances Derham held the chair of the group during this period. As an active member of both organisations, she attended InSEA World Council and World Congress meetings in Manila (1960) and Montreal (1963) as an Australian delegate.

Over the years, Derham continued collecting children's works of art; from children themselves, and through donations from colleagues throughout the world. The collection, amassed in the studio/garage of her home in Kew, Victoria, formed the basis of various exhibitions throughout Australia, the first of which she organised in 1937. The public responded very positively to seeing artworks by children in venues such as the Tasmanian Art Gallery in Hobart, the Athenaeum in Melbourne and Burt Memorial Hall in Perth. Several thousand visitors attended the exhibitions and the press took interest in discussing children's art in various city newspapers. Through her exhibitions, public lectures, radio talks and official advocacy for the reform of art education, Derham urged people to consider the importance of children's art.

Since the 1940s Derham had been searching for a home for her children's art collection
as part of a university or art museum. In 1975 she offered the collection to the Australian
National Gallery. In accepting her gift at that time, director James Mollison recognised the
special nature of the collection and its potential for research.

The collection chronicles diverse stories of childhood in the twentieth century and shows
how children around the world expressed their ideas through their art. Among the thousands
of works in collection are those of indigenous children at Hermannsburg (1938) and Aurukun
(1948) which portray children living in mission communities. As well, the collection includes
work by children who witnessed the Nazi rise to power in Austria, refugee children from the
Spanish Civil War and those experiencing inter-country conflict in Europe in the 1930s and 1940s.
Alongside these, Derham collected many thousands of Australian children's drawings from the
1930s to 1980s, depicting events such as Royal visits, the 1956 Olympics and everyday activities
in children's lives in a pre-television era.

Frances Derham retired from full-time work in the 1960s but her diaries indicate that she
maintained her professional commitments until very late in life. She also kept up her regular
drawing and painting routines, but in the later years mainly devoted herself to sorting,
organising and documenting the piles of children's art in her studio/garage. The gift in 1976
was the start of a long process of cataloguing and shipping the works to the National Gallery
in Canberra. In 1981 Derham held her last exhibition of children's art in Melbourne and wrote
a catalogue for the exhibition which summarised her philosophy of education through the arts.
When she packed up the display, she dispatched it to Canberra , thus marking the end of an
impressive record of collecting and exhibiting children's art. Derham died in 1987, aged 92.

Since the donation, the Frances Derham Collection has been housed at the National Gallery
of Australia. It has served as a subject of research for various scholars and parts of the collection
have been exhibited in Canberra (1984) and Sydney (1979 and 1997).

Hence, Derham's dream to have children's work become part of our cultural history
became reality. It is the task of the National Gallery of Australia to ensure that her work
and that of the children continues to benefit scholars and the community for whom she worked
so tirelessly.

Barbara Piscitelli

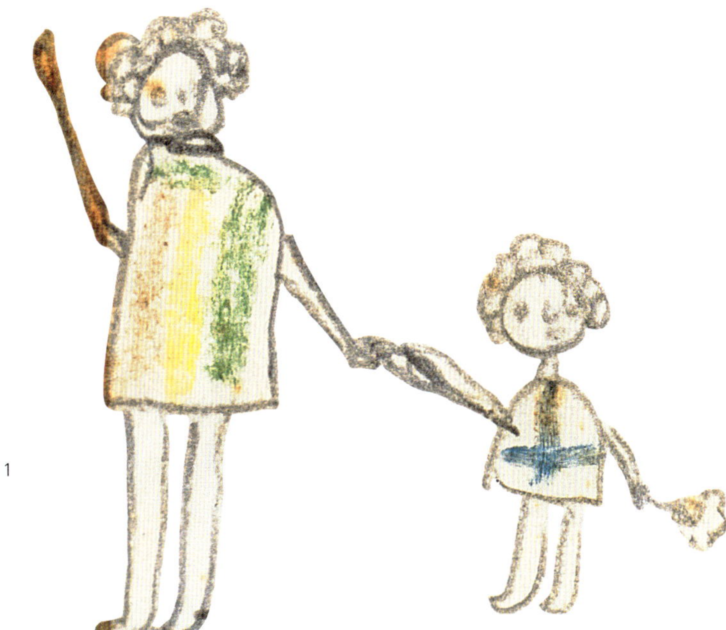

(opposite) **Frances Derham** *Moonlight* 1911
National Gallery of Australia

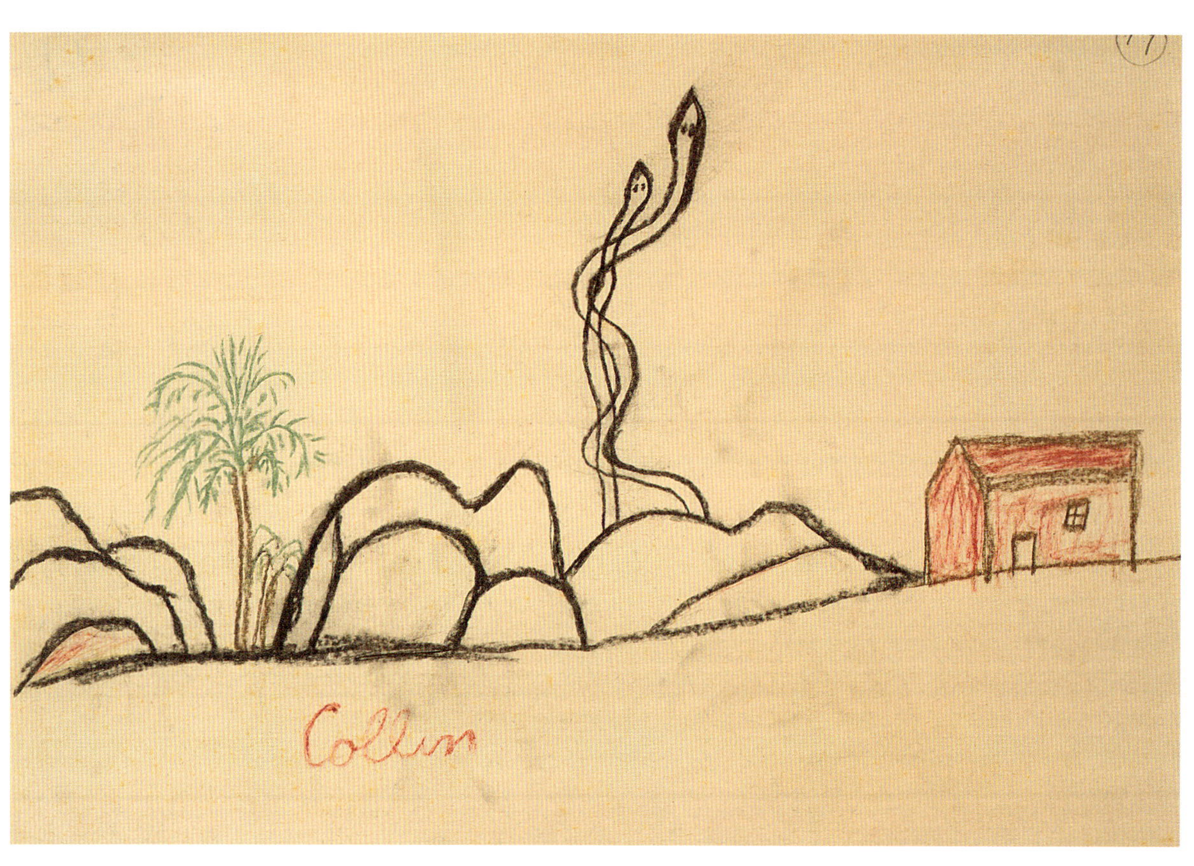

Collin Australia, Hermannsburg *Landscape with rainbow snakes* 1938

FRUITS OF THE GARDEN
Developments in children's art during the twentieth century

In *Childhoods Past* we see a collection of children's paintings and drawings that are the fruits of Frances Derham's adult life spent studying children's art, promoting children's issues, and educating future teachers to continue her work. Derham drew around her teachers, former students, artists and art educators interested in developing her ideas on teaching art to children. Many of these people had been educated in the principles and practice of Friedrich Fröebel, the nineteenth century German educator whose term 'kindergarten' or children's garden was also a metaphor for the relationship of the child as a plant, to the teacher as a gardener. Fröebel's kindergarten profoundly changed the perception of children as passive recipients of information and skills to that of active explorers of ideas. Fröebel explained his intention:

> *Little children … ought not to be schooled and taught, they need merely to be developed.*
> *It is the pressing need of our age, and only the idea of a garden can serve to show us symbolically …*
> *the proper treatment of children.*[1]

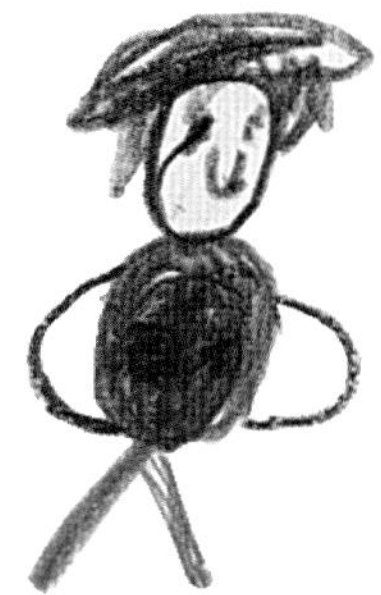

Student teachers at the Kindergarten Training Colleges in Australia in the early twentieth century studied the work of Fröebel and practiced using his twenty Gifts and Occupations, the materials and experiences he designed for young children. Fröebel's background as a scientist specialising in crystallography was influential in his conception of the Gifts and Occupations, through which he sought to convey the beauty and complexity of the natural world.

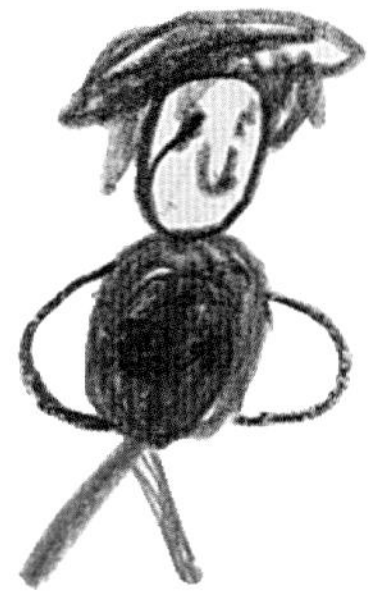

Fröebel's philosophy can be linked through several educators, including American educator and philosopher John Dewey, to the progressive education tradition which, during the mid twentieth century, brought about the perception of the child as an active learner, particularly in the arts. The emphasis on practical experiences in progressive education opened the way for the involvement of artist–educators in schools and teachers' colleges. By the 1920s and 1930s many notable artist–teachers, such as Marion Richardson in England and Franz Cizek in Vienna, were advocating changes in art education. By seeking to focus on the personal experience of children in creating art, they not only sought to validate children's work but drew the attention of adult artists to its qualities. Both Richardson and Cizek influenced practices in Australia through the work of Frances Derham and others.

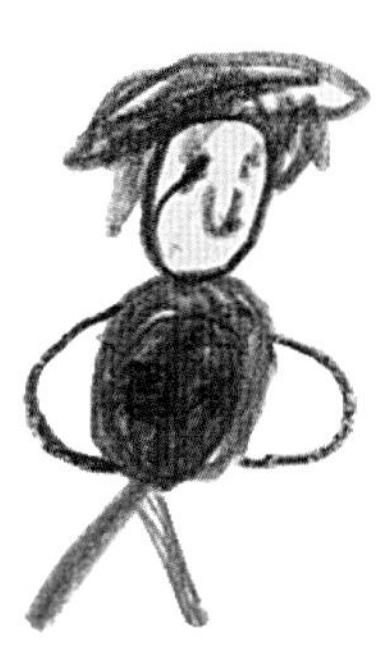

Parallels between Richardson and Derham are of particular interest. Richardson was one of the main critics of the South Kensington system, a carefully prescribed system of art education originally intended to equip students for the uniform design and crafting of goods in newly-industrialised England in the late nineteenth and early twentieth centuries. Richardson believed that children needed freedom to explore experiences relevant to their daily lives and to know the pleasure of communicating through art. This contrasted strongly with the South Kensington approach — which was the first system of art education that Derham experienced as a child in New Zealand, and which she later discarded as a teacher.

Richardson's practice was inextricably linked with the New Education movement and her innovations, including her approach to handwriting, were passed on through the networks of the New Education Fellowship (NEF) in England, Europe and Japan, and the Progressive Education Association (PEA) in America. These groups saw the need to develop new educational theories and practices in response to the rapid social, political and scientific changes that were taking place. They were concerned to create new opportunities based

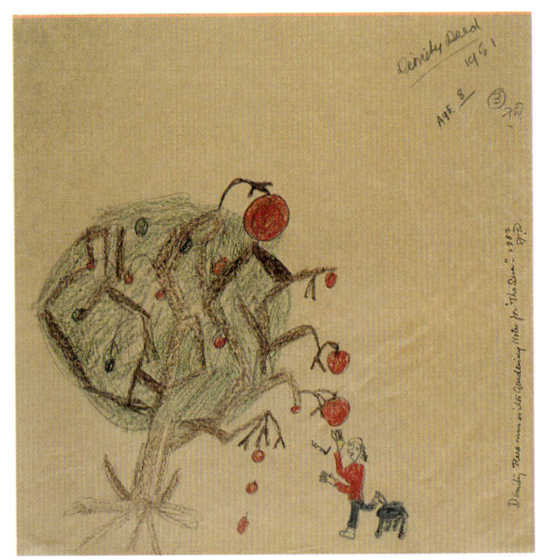

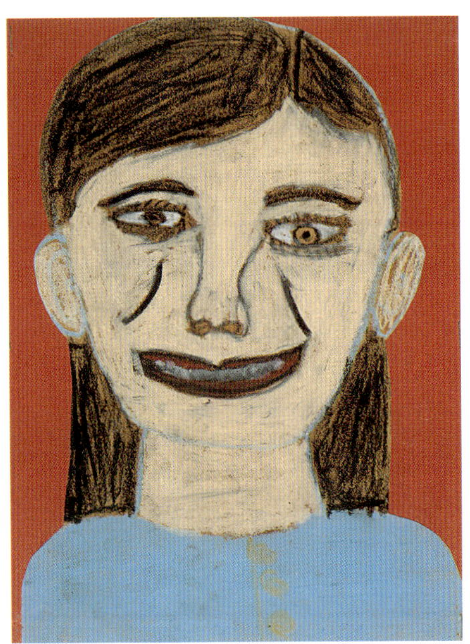

(above top) **Dimity Reed**
Australia, Melbourne
Reach for the apple 1951

(above) **Sarah**
Canada Inuit
Self-portrait 1963

on an understanding of the whole child rather than the intellect alone, and to encompass the human spirit in an era of technological change.

In embracing her new awareness of individual expression in art, Richardson explored the contrast in practice between drawing from direct observation and from memory. It has been suggested that her background in Christian Science contributed to her interest in visualised mental images. Derham's interest in individual expression appears to have come more directly from her study of developments in psychology, through her work with colleagues at Preshil school and the Melbourne Kindergarten Training College and through the networks of the NEF and PEA.

In April 1938 the Australian Commonwealth Government decided to fund demonstration Nursery–Kindergarten centres in each state. These were named after Lady Gowrie, wife of the Governor General at the time, in recognition for her contribution to the scheme. The centres provided a model for early childhood practice and facilitated scientific research into all areas of children's development. Derham was closely involved with the Melbourne centre and undertook research into aspects of children's artistic development.

An example of her research was the Reach for the Apple test. This was based on a similar test developed by Viennese psychologist and art education writer, Viktor Lowenfeld in 1939, and outlined in his book *The Nature of Creative Activity*. The book was translated from German by the Melbourne analyst and scholar Oscar Oeser who was known to Derham through her connection with Preshil school.

Lowenfeld gave a detailed outline of the problem he set the children: The topic was:

… you are under an apple tree. On one of its lower branches you see an apple which you particularly admire and which you would like to have. You stretch out your hand to pick the apple, but your reach is just about a span too short. Then you make a great effort and get the apple after all. Now you have it and enjoy eating it. Draw yourself as you are taking the apple off the tree.[2]

Derham undertook the test in different settings with a large number of children. The test was designed to study differences in children's drawings according to two particular personality 'types' that Lowenfeld identified. In her book, *Art for the Child Under Seven*, Derham outlines this difference as:

objective (visual) — as if seen by a spectator — or subjective (haptic), a creation of his thoughts and feelings about something that has interested him and in which he feels involved.[3]

Her goal was to show the importance of individual differences between children and to outline ways of encouraging artistic development, regardless of a child's predisposition to create recognisable images.

From the 1930s, psychologists' interest in children's art as a mirror of human development was parallelled by Modernist artists' interest in Outsider Art and Art Brut. These terms embraced the art of children, of so called 'primitive' people and of the 'mentally ill'. Such art was seen as spontaneous, unselfconscious, natural, and direct. Artists such as Picasso, Klee and Kandinsky were inspired by this art and in some cases incorporated the types of imagery it produced into their own works. Picasso is said to have stated that although as a child he could draw like Raphael, it took many years to be able to draw like a child.

The Modernist movement was the impetus for many exhibitions of children's art. The motivation to organise such exhibitions has frequently been associated with wider social and educational issues. Exhibitions provided a meeting place for the exchange of experience and ideas, as was the case in 1917 when Marion Richardson met art critic Roger Fry who held an exhibition of children's art at the Omega Workshops in London. Similarly, the relationship between art and psychoanalysis was the impetus for a 1944 exhibition of drawings and paintings by pupils of A.S. Neill's school Summerhill at the Arcade Gallery in London. Post-war emphasis on education for international understanding gave rise to some significant exhibitions. A particularly poignant collection of children's art, exhibited in many countries since the end of World War II, is that of the children of the Terezin ghetto in Northern Bohemia, most of them on the way to Nazi extermination camps. A collection of children's paintings titled Unteilbares Deutchland (Germany Indivisible) created in 1961 also offered a powerful political message.[4] Here, the hopes for the reunification of Germany were the basis of the images, many of which anticipated the destruction of the Berlin Wall.

In recent decades, social changes such as greater cultural diversity, developments in information and communication technologies, and increasingly global perspectives have come to influence the way children's art is perceived. With the awareness that today's young will inhabit a world that is likely to differ markedly from the present, qualities such as flexibility, resilience, autonomy, co-operation are highly valued for their potential to enable children to generate new ideas, to take risks and share understanding and ideas with others.

Creative arts experiences can enrich children's lives and enable them to communicate in a range of media. They can also provide valuable opportunities for imagining the future and skills to help children put their ideas into practice. Increasingly, the valuable insights gained into children's artistic development during the twentieth century are being used to create environments that reflect qualities such as respect for different ideas and forms of expression. Rather than seeing one single method of art education as 'correct', teachers and parents are encouraged to develop their own skills and insights to help them become discerning in the choices they make for the children in their care.

In this exhibition viewers have the opportunity to reflect on their emotional responses, not only to the children's art, but to their own childhood. That these images have survived to be celebrated in this way is a tribute to a human thread which reaches over the twentieth century, a constellation of communities which has included artists, educators, parents, academics, gallery curators and administrators and a myriad of viewers who have brought genuine emotional response to the art of children. It would seem to be of the utmost priority that adults draw on their ability to recall their own childhood and in valuing that, ensure that the childhood of our children is filled with opportunities to express wonder and curiosity in imaginative and dynamic ways through art.

Margaret White

1   Friedrich Fröebel, *Letters on the Kindergarten*, London: Swan, Sonnenschein, 1891.

2   Viktor Lowenfeld, *The Nature of Creative Activity*, London: Routledge and Kegan Paul, 1939, p.72.

3   Frances Derham, *Art for the Child Under Seven*, Canberra: Australian Preschool Association, 1973 edn, p.12.

4   W. Schultz, *Unteilbares Deutchland Kuratorium*, n.p., 1961.

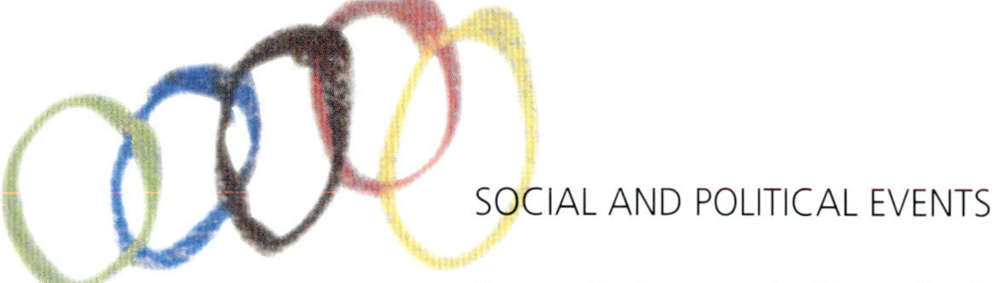

Frances Derham acquired her collection through donations from various sources and by soliciting drawings from children in schools around the world. A significant collection of drawings and paintings from the Progressive Education Association was brought to Australia in the late 1930s. This important exhibition contained work from children on five continents and had been travelling around the world for several years prior to its arrival in Australia. Within the collection were numerous works that documented children's social and political lives, showing the events and issues that children encountered during the worldwide Great Depression and the global conflict in the 1930s.

Frances Derham immediately saw the important messages contained in the children's images and displayed their works in Sydney, Melbourne, Adelaide, Hobart and Perth from 1938 to 1942. The exhibitions drew thousands of visitors and were reported widely in the media, with claims that children everywhere should be given freedom to depict their ideas through the visual arts.

The Progressive Education Association disbanded while its exhibition was in Australia, so Frances Derham retained the children's art for posterity. Through her exposure of the works, and her radio broadcasts about children and their art, she became well known and often received unsolicited donations of children's art. Over her lifetime, Frances Derham built a substantial collection of work from Australia and these depicted the unique environment and lifestyle of the country. Her collection was drawn from various schools, kindergartens and studio programs in urban, rural and remote areas. Among the many thousands of images in her collection are some that depict special events such as the 1956 Melbourne Olympics and the 1960 Royal visit.

War

The impact of war on children's lives should not be underestimated. Children use drawing to document their feelings and views on events they observe. On the European front during World War II, children drew their impressions of bombs dropping and the ruin of their social worlds. Young children from the northern Italian Montessori School Casa Dei Bambini used tiny paper and delicate coloured pencils to portray the destruction of their community as bombs fell on their churches, mountain villages and families. Spanish children from a French refugee camp drew images which showed the ruins of their homes and the resulting humanitarian efforts to assist the wounded and displaced. In Austria, children watched the changing of their nation as a new regime raised flags, and graphically recorded the development of a new social order.

Changing social order

During the Great Depression, children chronicled the changing social order with images of unemployment, child labour, poverty and family upheaval. Changes to the environment also form part of the visual inventory for children's representations and they often record the development of architectural and engineering feats, see for example the drawing of the Panama Canal, page 24.

Special events

Art lessons in most schools involve children in making pictures about special events and class excursions. In this way, children become socialised in the art of illustrating their lives. During the 1956 Melbourne Olympics, children were eager spectators as Lorraine Crapp swam for Australia. They took interest in the new sporting facilities and the arrival of the Olympic torch to their city. When the new Queen visited Australia in 1960, one Melbourne school child painted her departure on the large plane, with the story, 'She's going away'. In 1942, the arrival of a large passenger ship in Melbourne provided the visual prompt for a child to record his memory of the excursion.

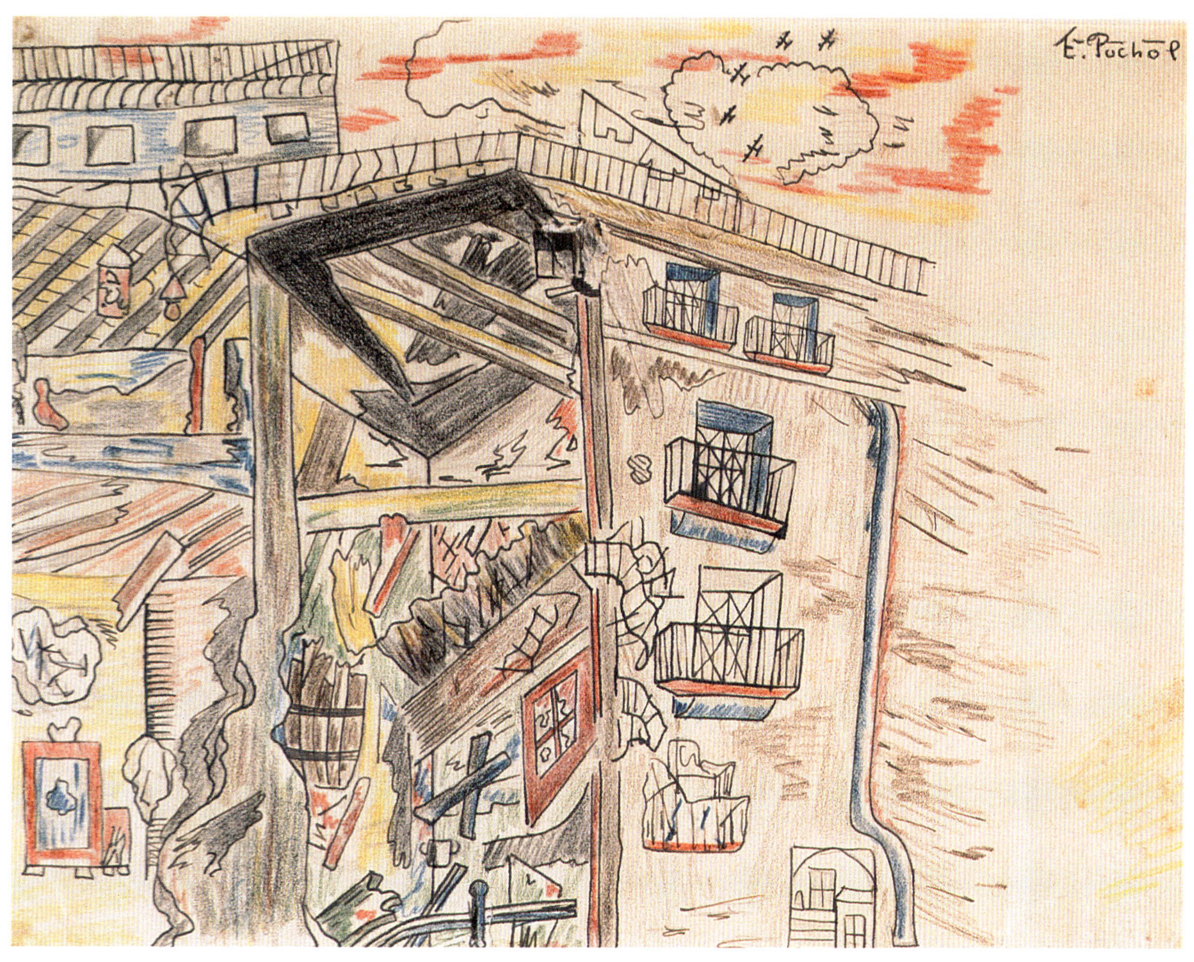

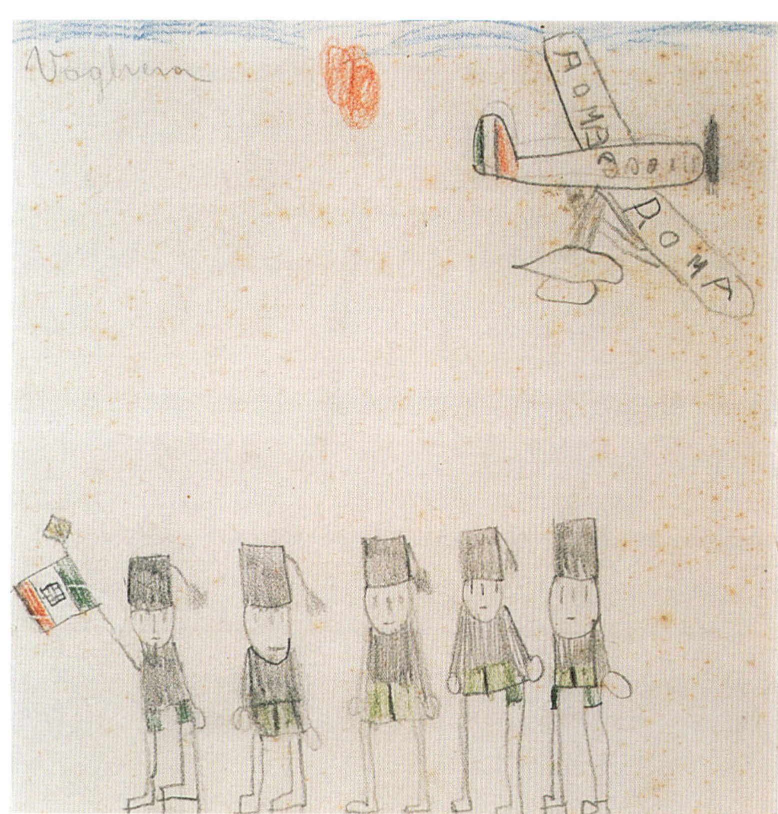

(above) **E. Puchol**
Spain
Bombed building
c.1930

(right) **Voghera**
Italy
Plane and soldiers
c.1930

Dahmke

Malo -IVB- 10años
Material de
G. y Huaka
nor me
Escuela Justo Arosemena
PANAMA.

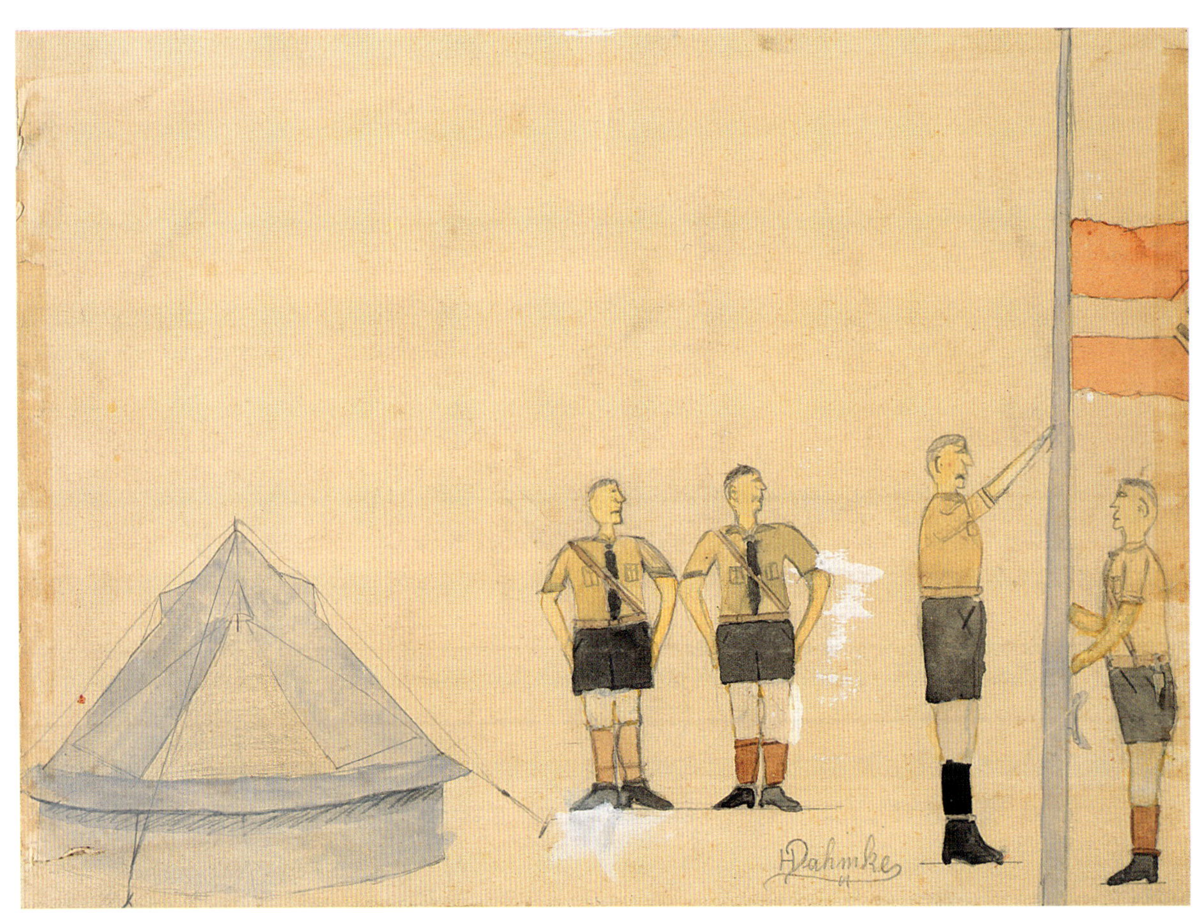

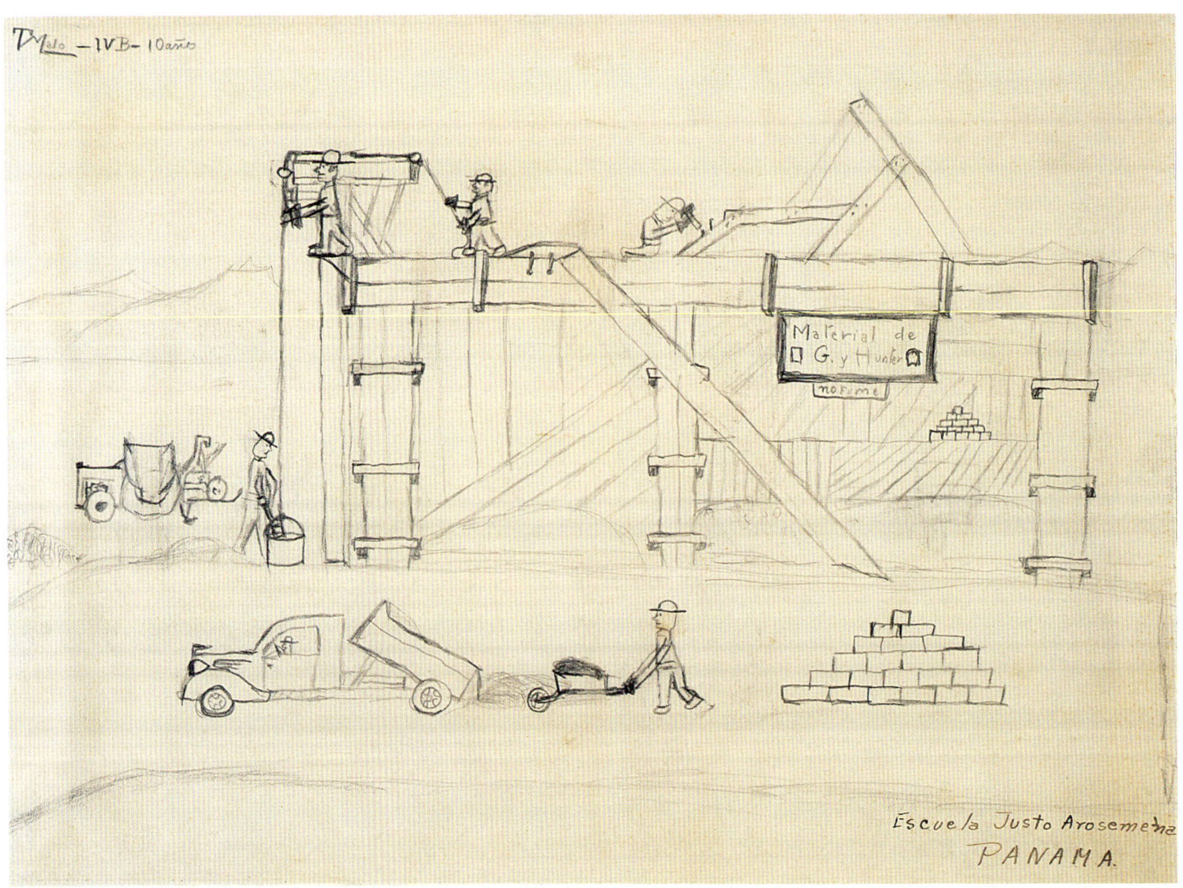

24

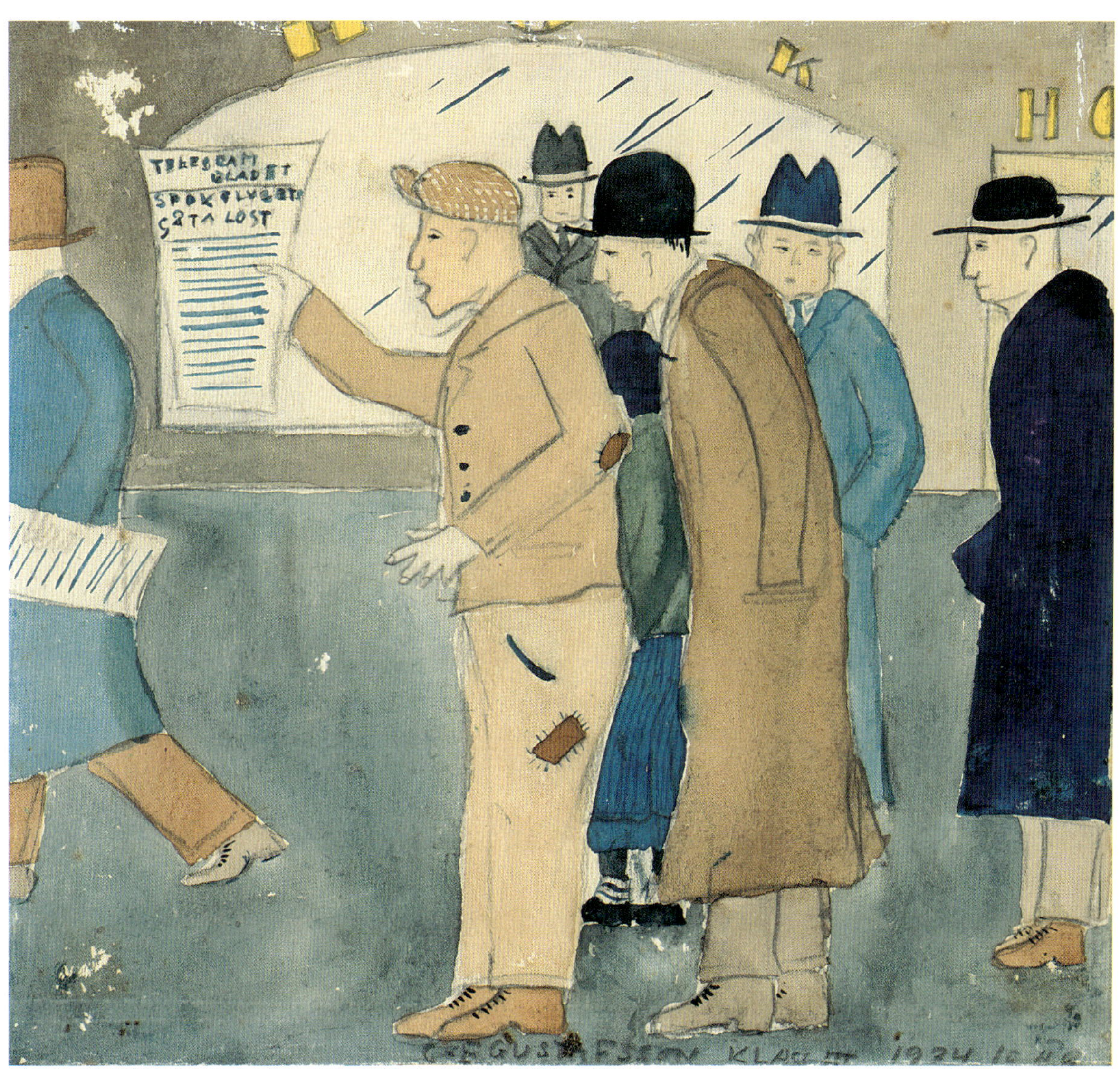

(above) **C.E. Gustafsson** Finland *Depression* 1934
(opposite above) **H. Dahrike** Austria *Raising the flag* c.1930
(opposite below) **T. Malo** Central America *Building of the Panama Canal* c.1930

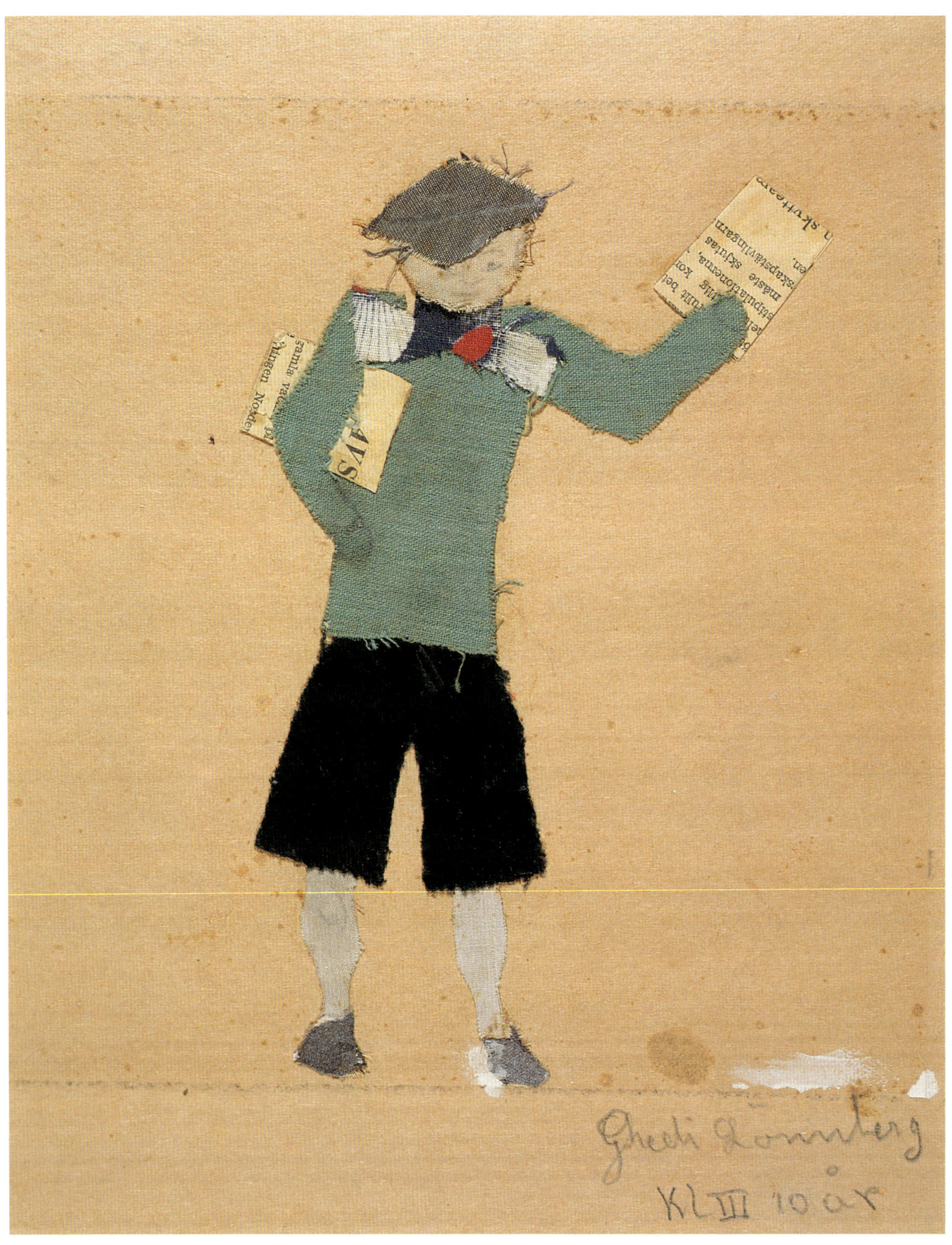
AVS

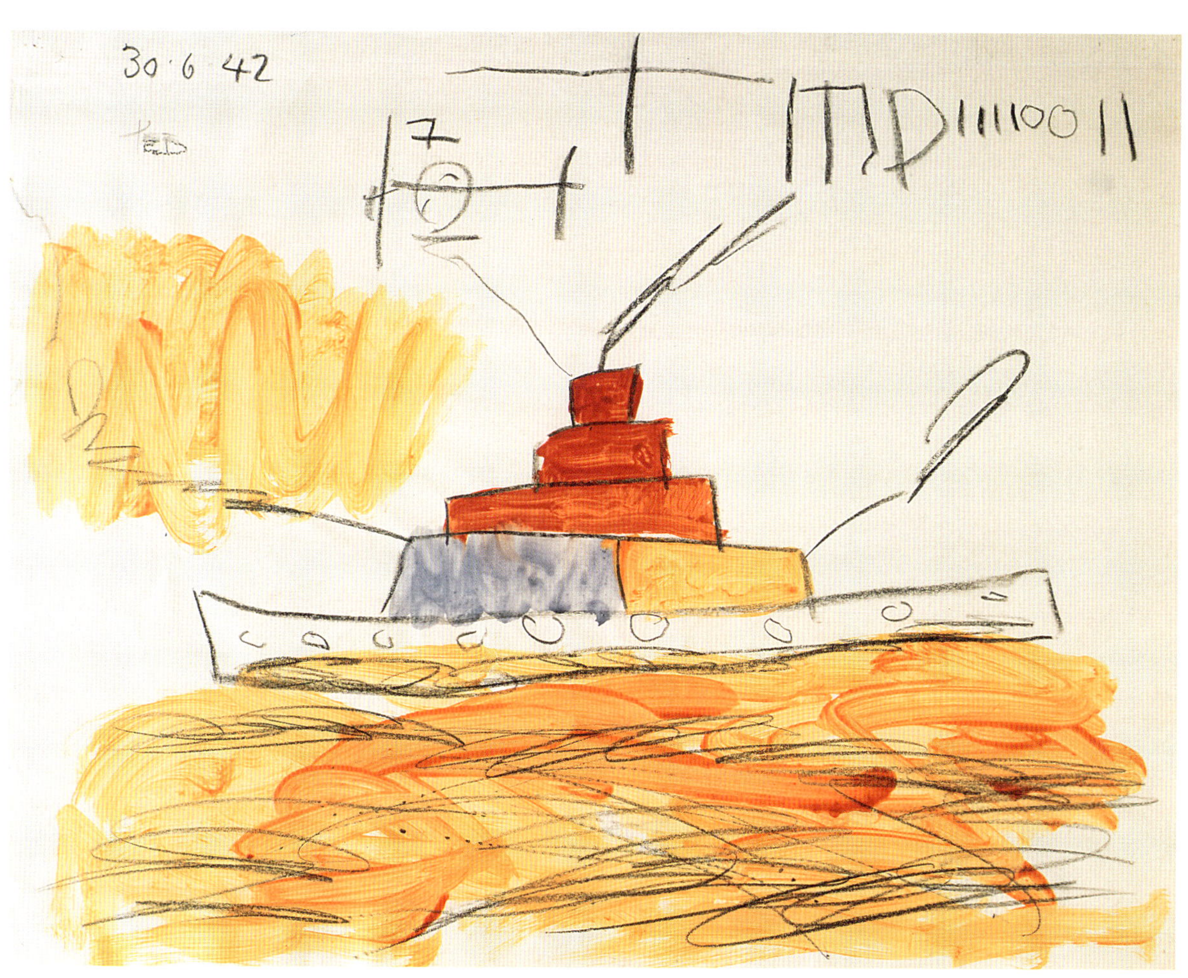

(above) **Ted** Australia, Melbourne *Ship* 1942
(opposite) **Gheeli Sonnberg** Finland *Paper boy* c.1930

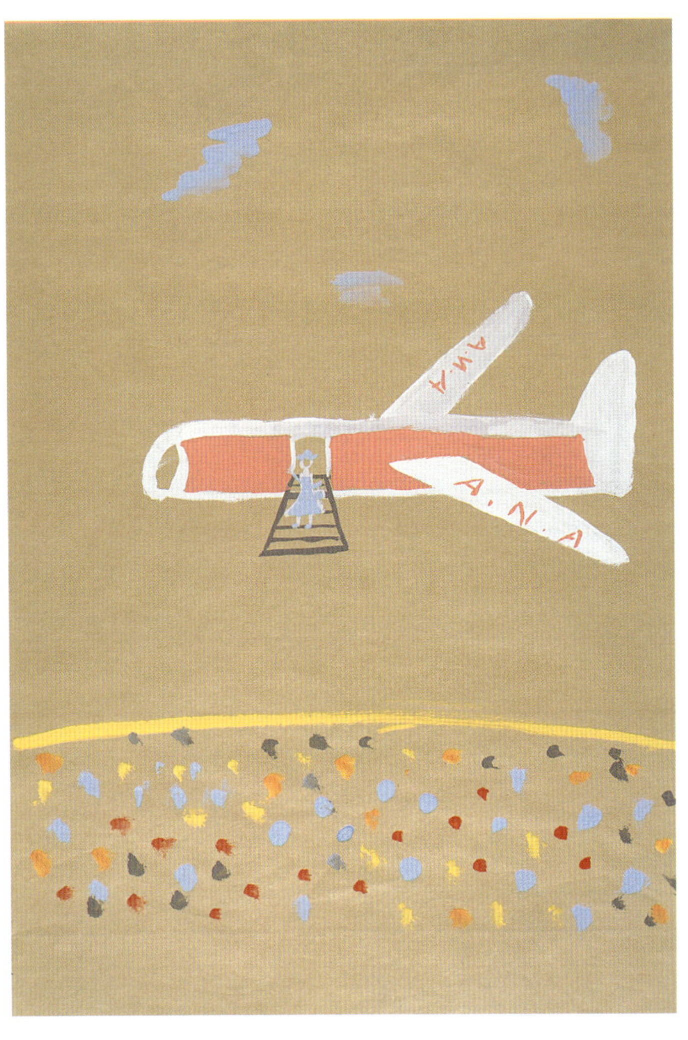

(left) **Jamie Cumming**
Australia, Melbourne
Someone climbing (She's going away) 1960

(below left) **Unknown**
Australia, Melbourne
Olympic torch 1956

(opposite above) **Antony Baillieu**
Australia, Melbourne
Olympic swimming pool 1956

(opposite below) **P. Baxter**
Australia, Melbourne
Come on Lorraine Crapp 1956

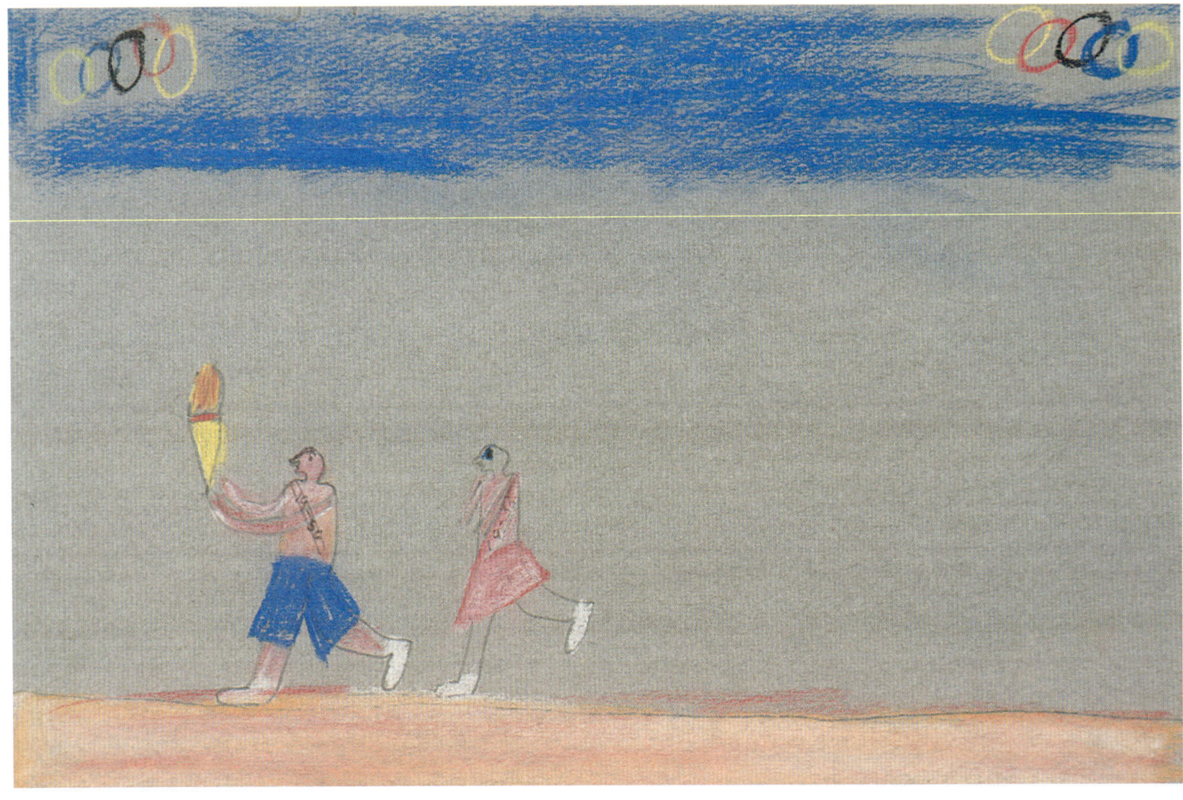

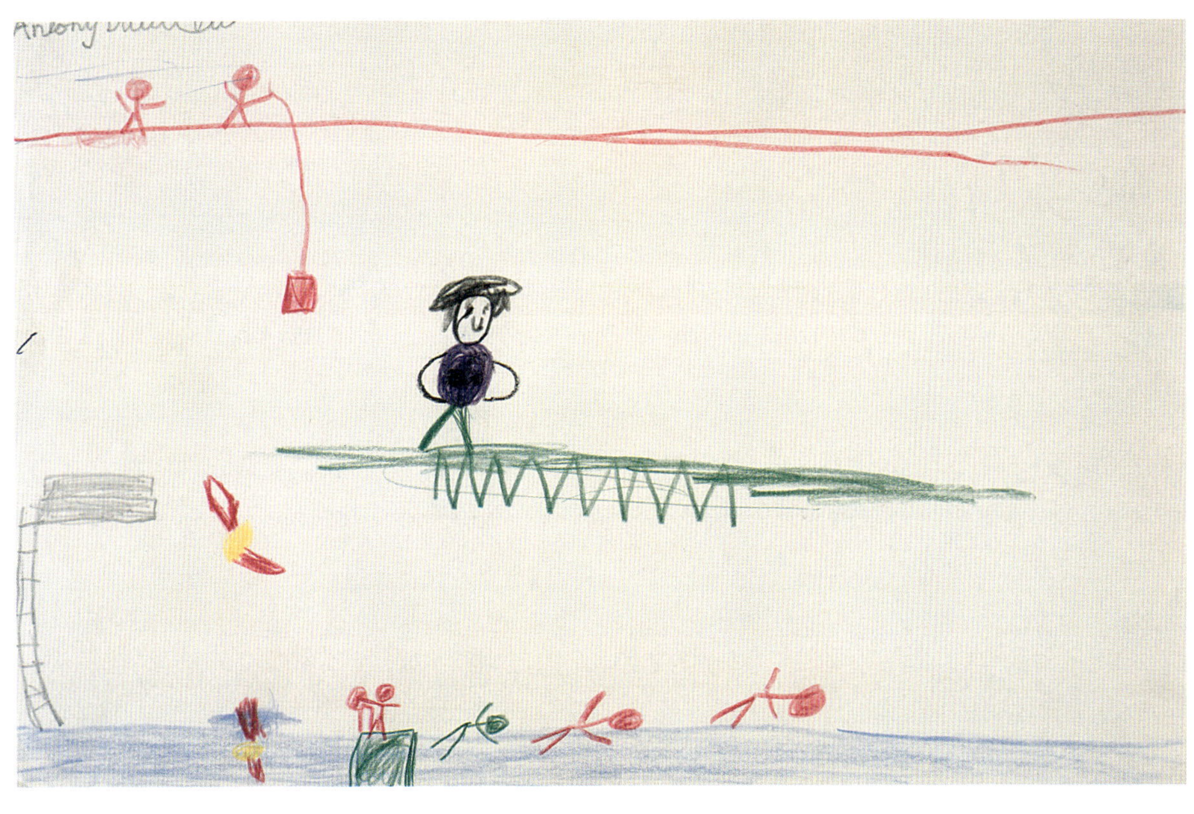

Anthony

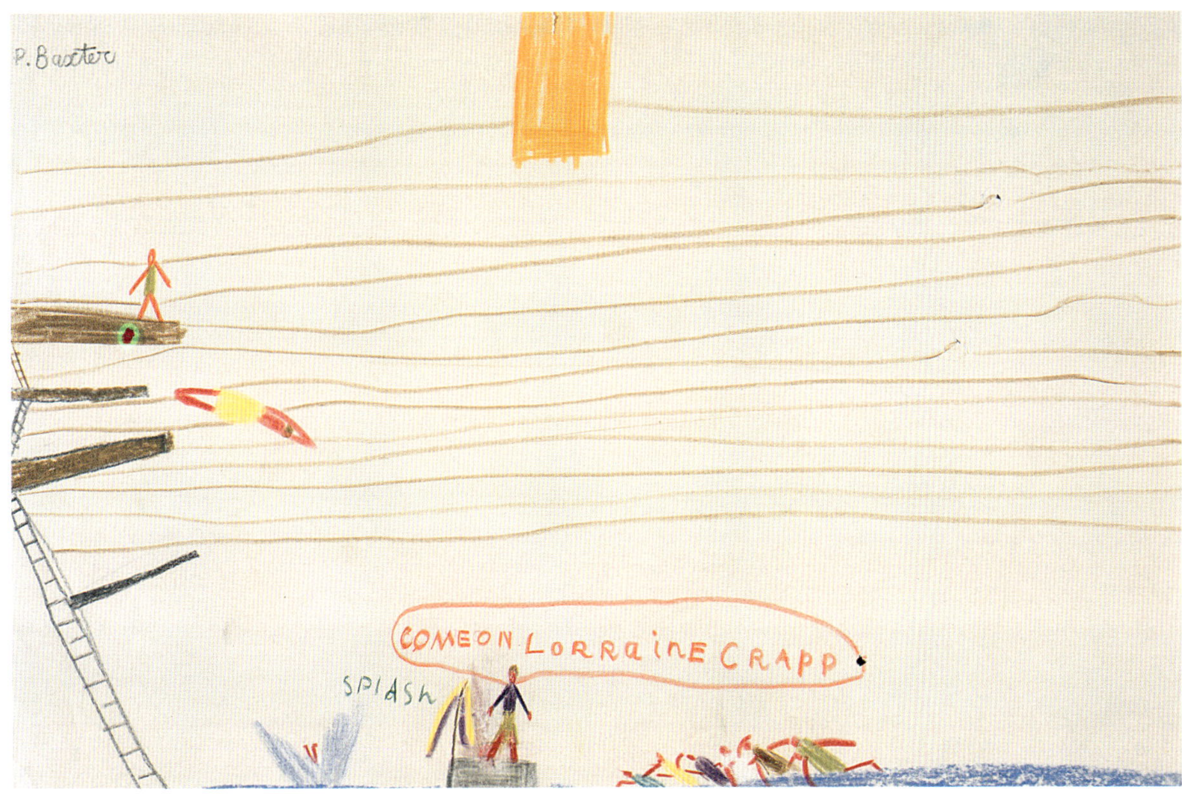

P. Baxter
COME ON LORRAINE CRAPP
SPLASH

PERSONAL AND CULTURAL IDENTITY

Like all artists, children reveal their personal and cultural identity through their drawings
and paintings. The great diversity of human experience is contained within their graphic
representations — in self and family portraits, landscapes and cityscapes, daily routines
and special celebrations. Within *Childhoods Past*, children present a range of urban and rural
activity, including everyday events such as waiting for the mail, preparing a meal, going
to school, hunting and mustering. In their art children capture the detail of both commonplace
and extraordinary events as an important record of their views about life. Children are often
forgotten and neglected as commentators in the larger world but their pictures are a poignant
reminder that they are observant and involved members of society.

Over the course of the twentieth century, Frances Derham sought out work to represent
the diversity of life. The Eurocentric focus of her early collection was balanced by the acquisition
of work from indigenous groups. Derham's journeys to central Australia in 1938 and northern
Australia in 1948 afforded her the opportunity to work directly with Aboriginal children
in mission settlements. These trips were arduous with many days in transit by train or boat
to reach the remote communities of Hermannsburg and Aurukun. Once there, she supplied
drawing materials to children and held outdoor art classes.

Hermannsburg
In the 1930s Hermannsburg was a flourishing site for art. Children watched with interest
as Albert Namatjira painted watercolours of the strikingly beautiful landscape. When Frances
Derham provided the opportunity to make their own pictures, the children of Hermannsburg
recorded many of their favourite places and events. Not surprisingly, the children's images
mirrored the style and genre of work prominent among the adult artists in the community.

Aurukun
The remote coastal mission settlement of Aurukun was home for several indigenous peoples.
During her art classes in 1948, Frances Derham encouraged the children of Aurukun to depict
life on the mission. The range of images collected provides a glimpse into their life experiences
— going to church, pig hunting, picnicking, fishing, mustering.

Self-portrait
Faces form the first recognisable images in children's artistic repertoire. Over time children
become increasing adept at representing themselves in self-portraits.

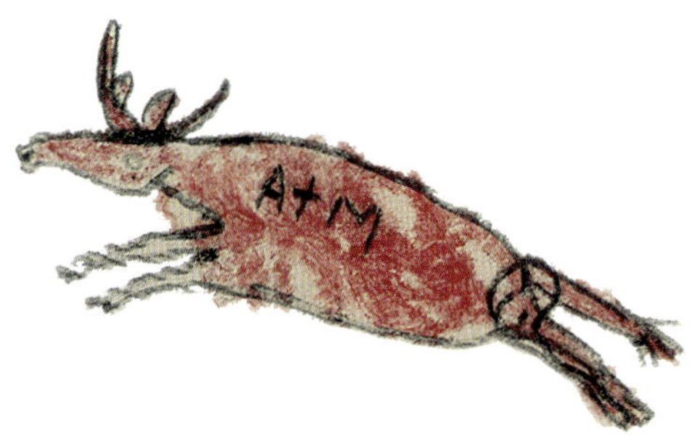

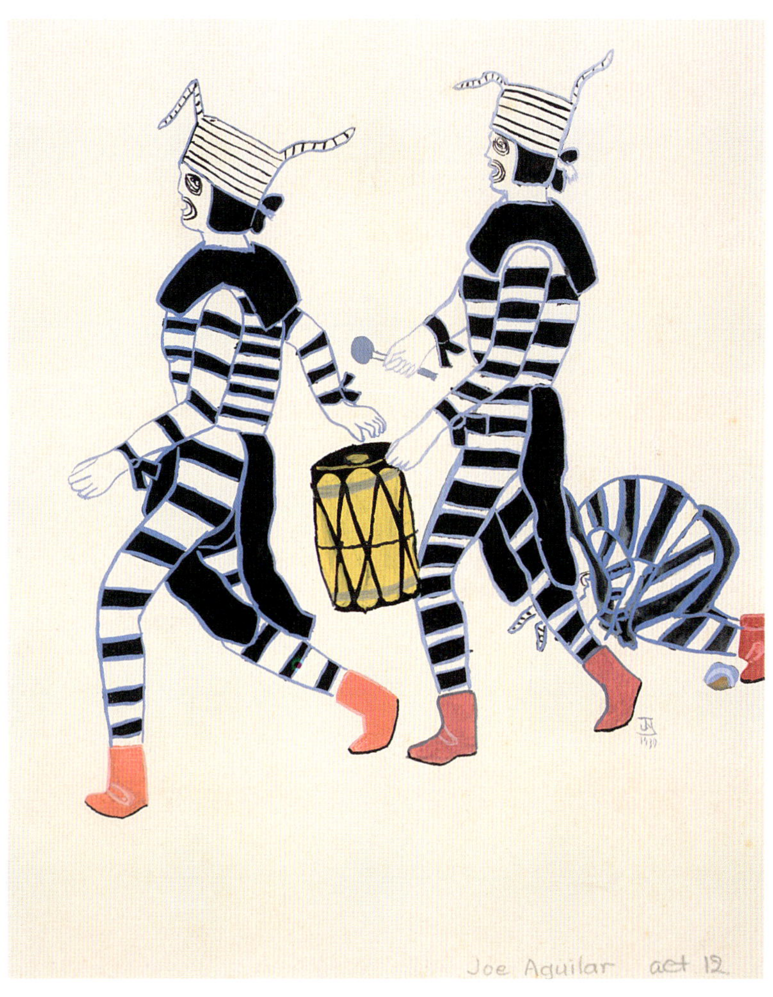

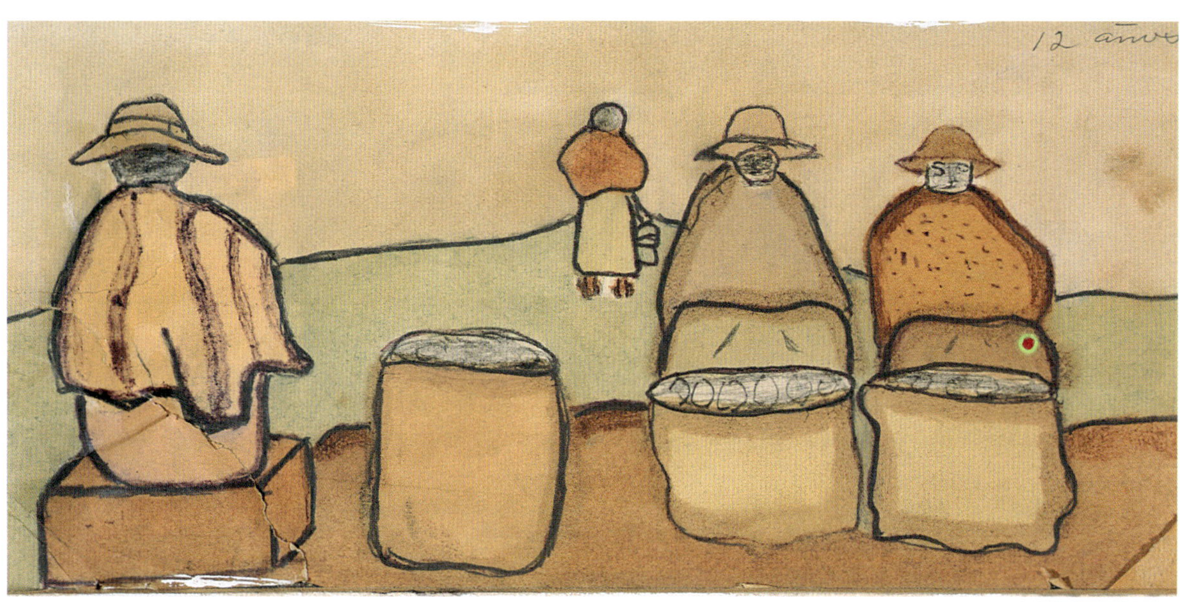

(above top) **Joe Aguilar** United States of America, Navajo *Three dancing figures with drum* c.1930
(above) **Quevedo** South America *Grain sellers* c.1930

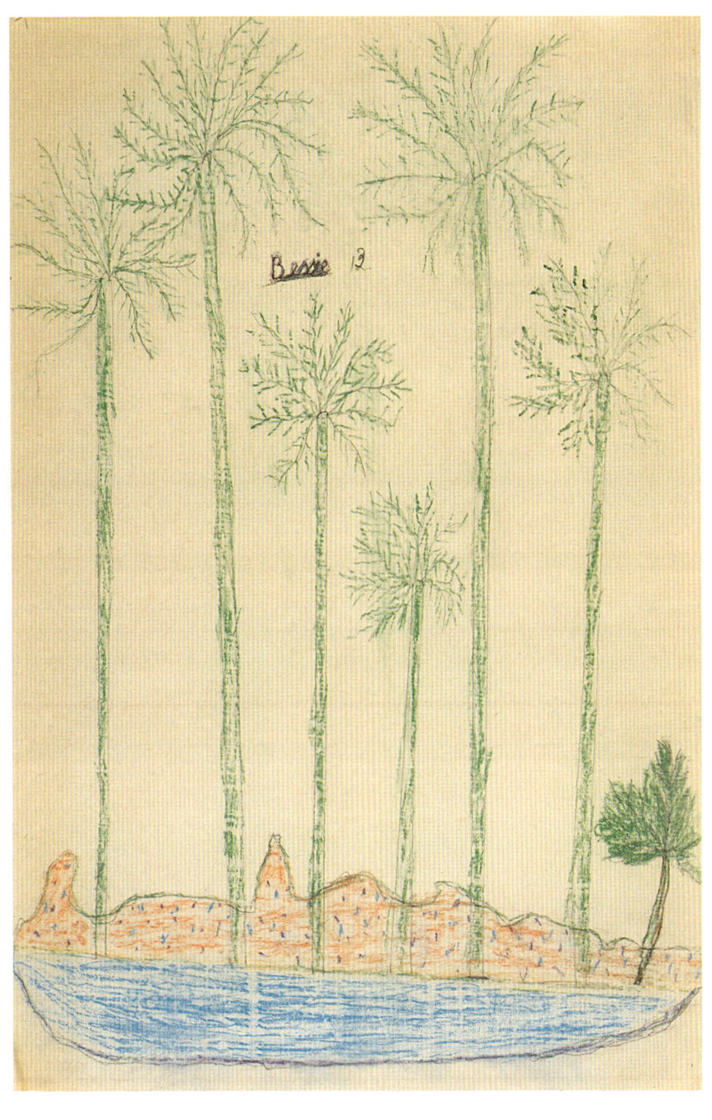

(left) **Bessie**
Australia, Hermannsburg
Palm Valley 1938

(below) **Claude Panka**
Australia, Hermannsburg
Aeroplane 1938

(opposite above) **Sailor Koomdtta**
Australia, Aurukun
Untitled 1948

(opposite below left) **Brian Pamtoonda**
Australia, Aurukun
Pig hunting 1948

(opposite below right) **Bobbie Kummara**
Australia, Aurukun
Stockmen mustering the cow 1948

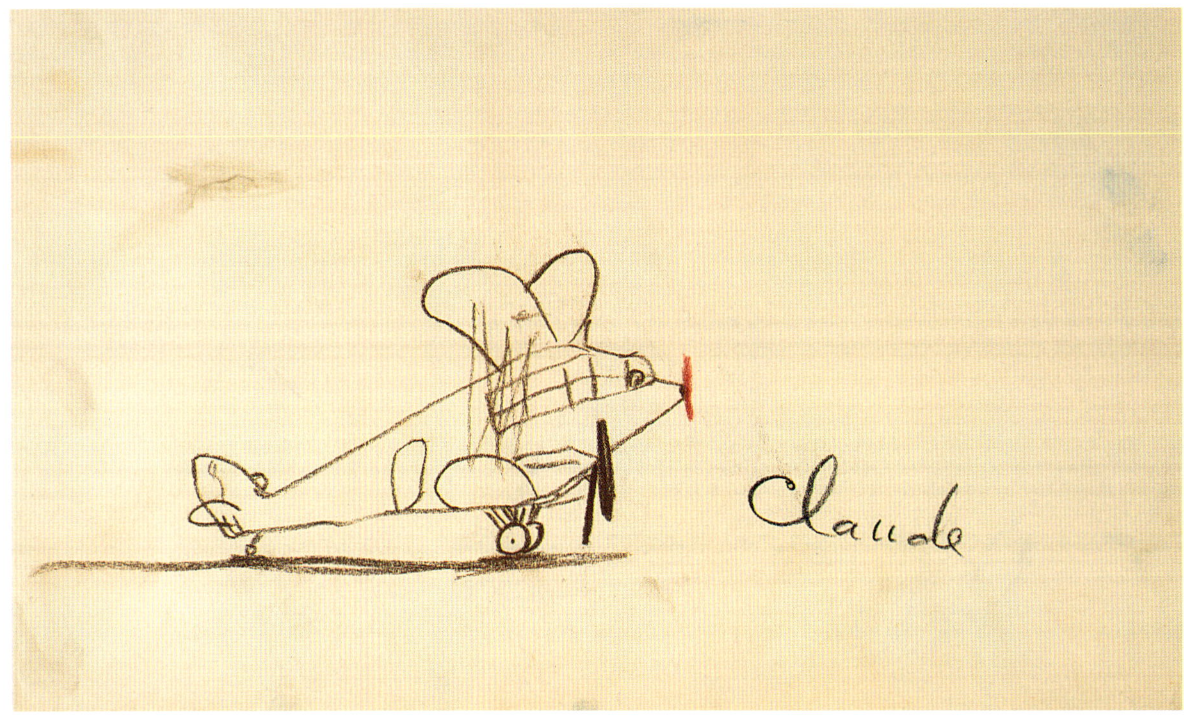

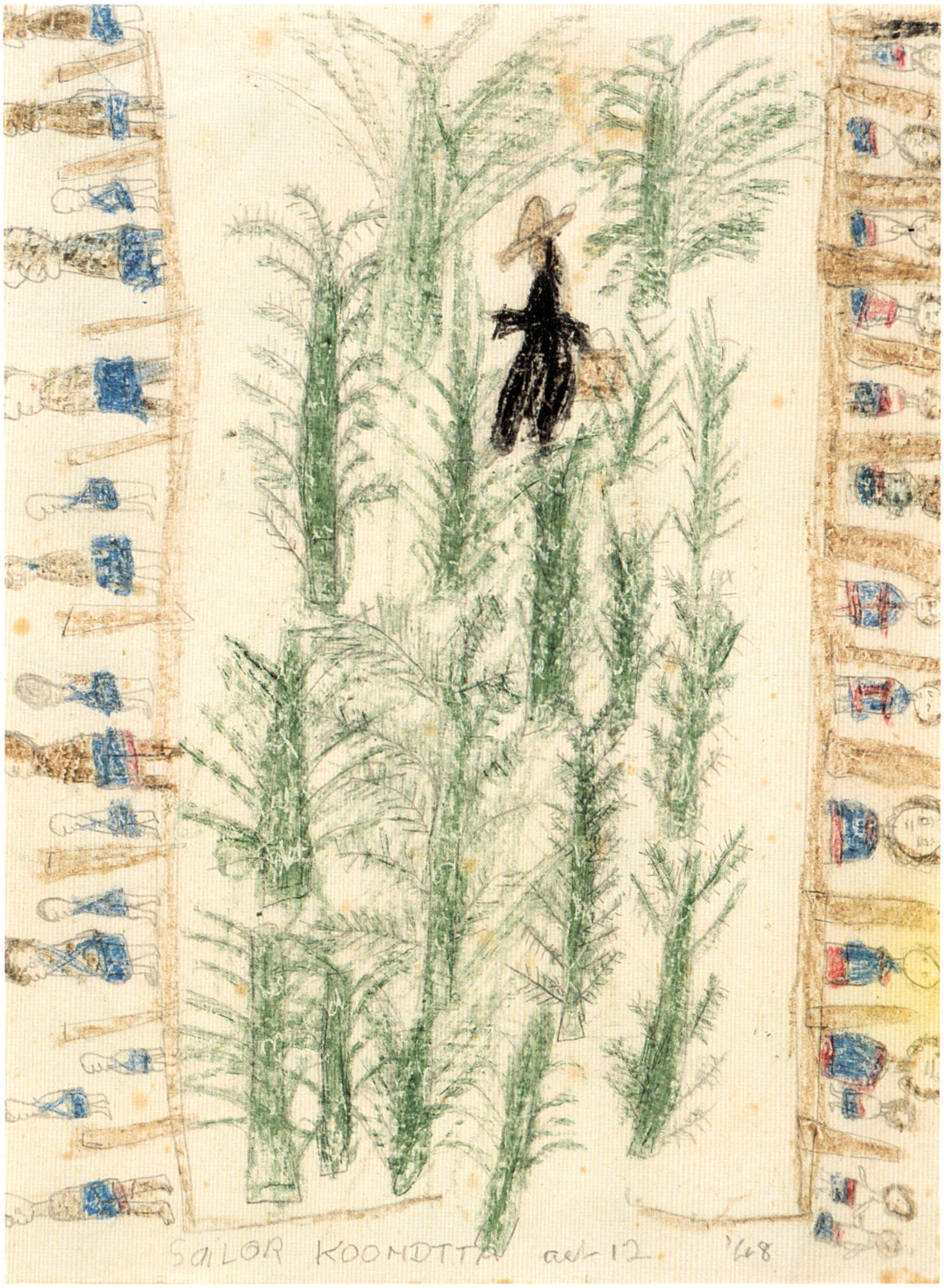

SAILOR KOONDTTA aet-12 '48

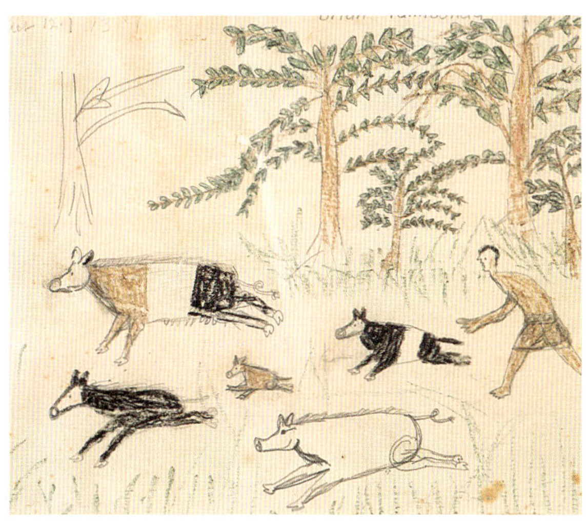

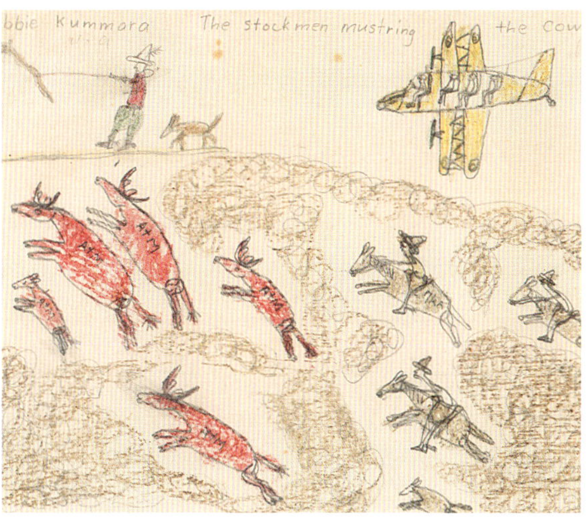

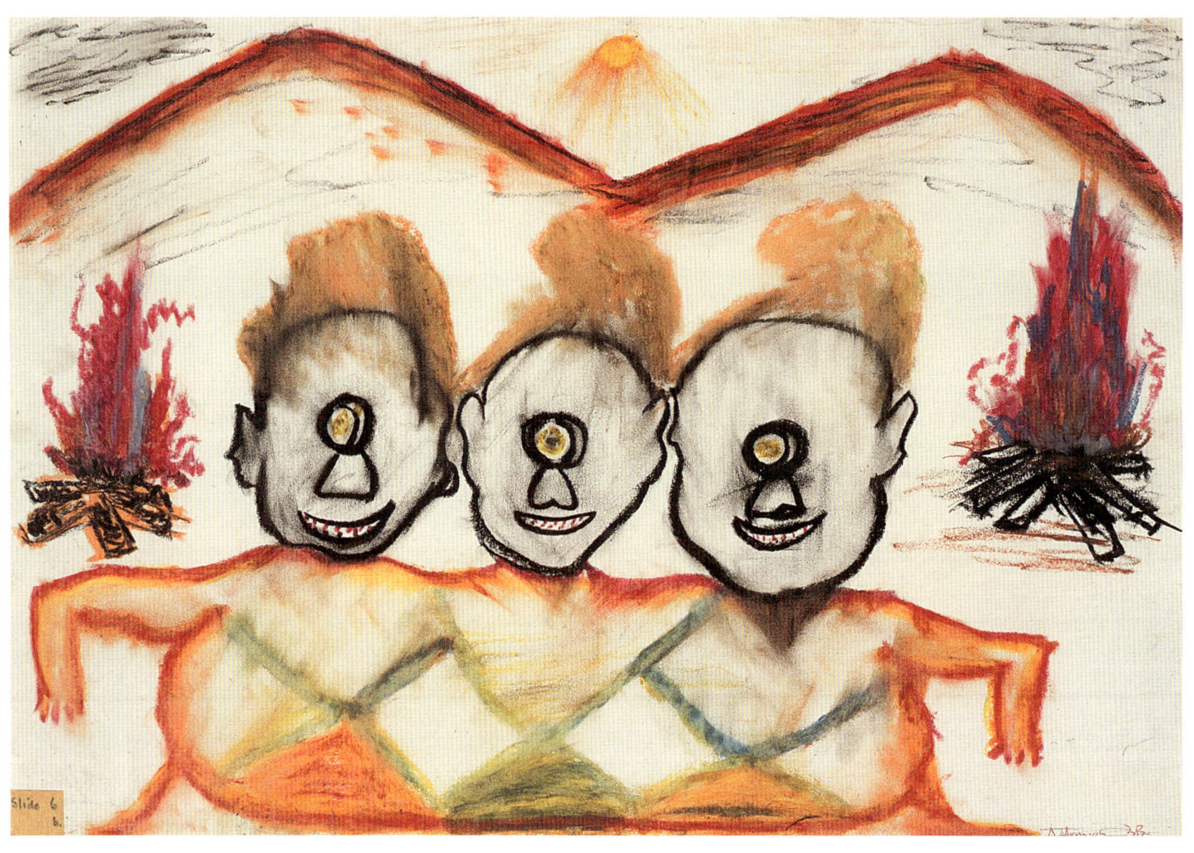

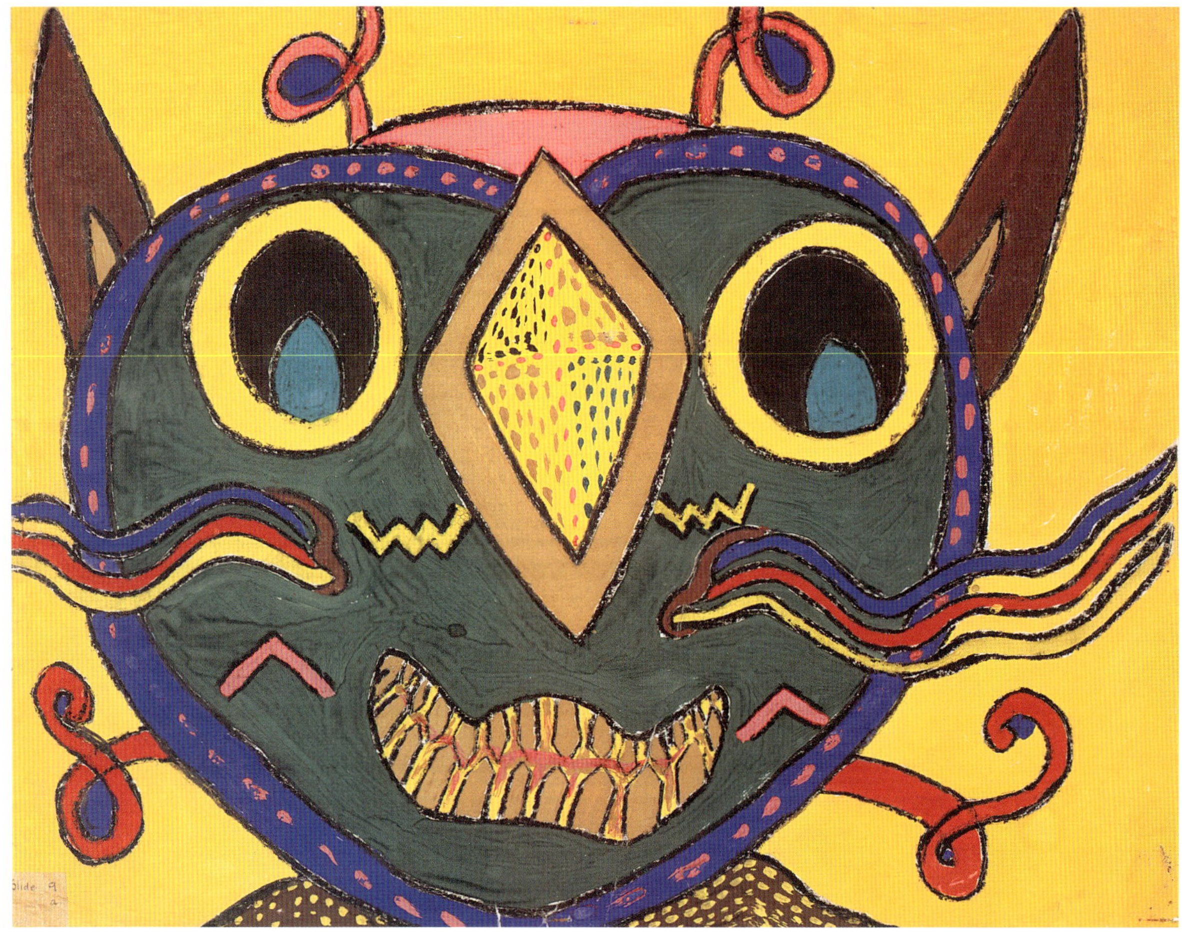

34

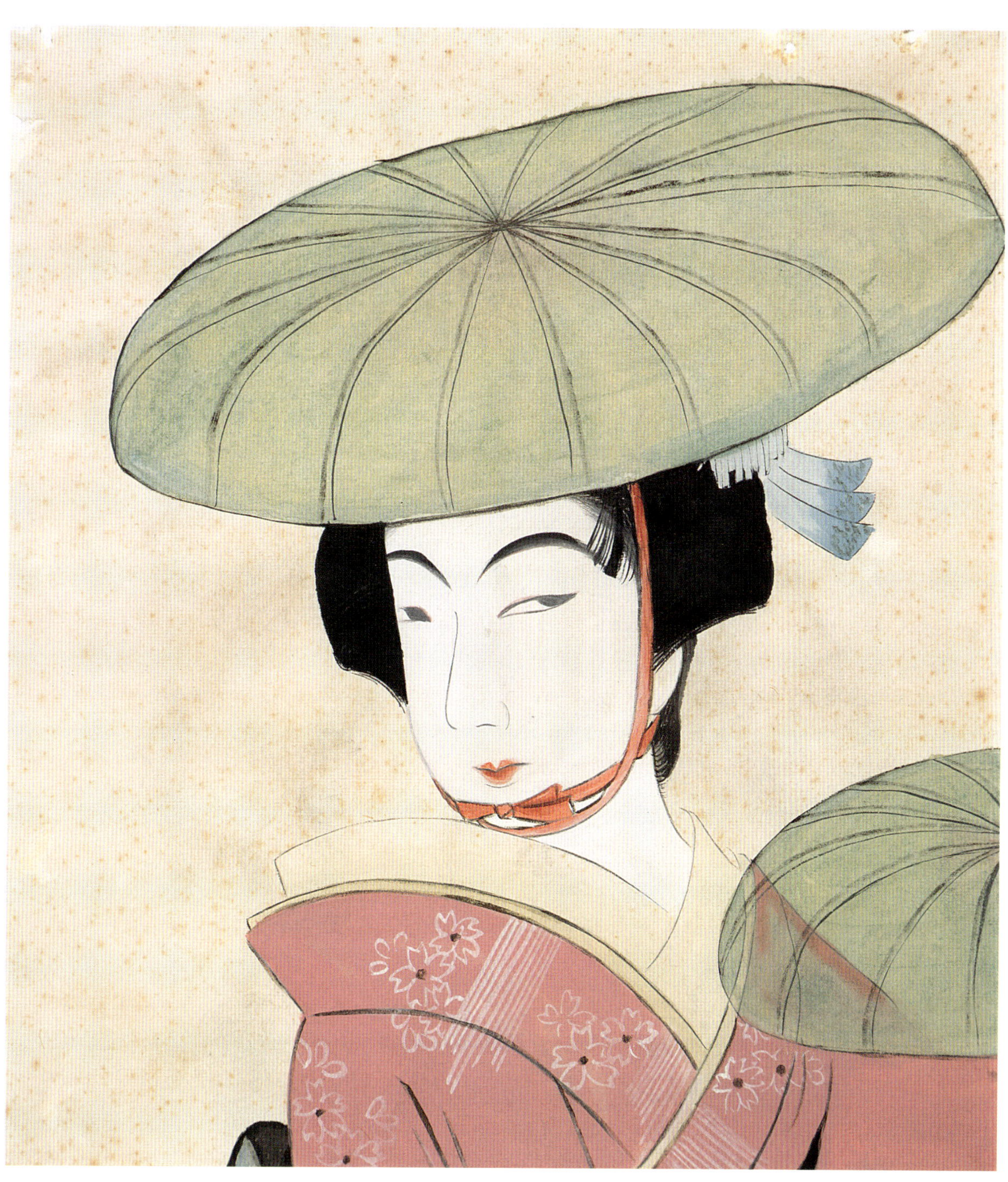

(above) **Takeshi Yamazaki** Japan *Woman in green hat* c.1930
(opposite above) **A. Monies** Papua New Guinea *Three headed monster* c.1967
(opposite below) **June Enock** Papua New Guinea, Malabunga, East New Britain Untitled c.1967

During the twentieth century, perceptions of the nature of learning relationships between children and teachers have changed significantly. For example, before Friedrich Fröebel's kindergarten practices became influential in the late nineteenth century, young children were often expected to sit for long periods of time in tiers of wooden benches with hands clasped together, listening to a teacher telling them about the world around them.

Fröebel's kindergarten profoundly changed such expectations as children were released both physically and metaphorically into 'gardens' where they experienced the world for themselves and interacted with the teacher whose role was closer to the Latin derivation of education, *educare*, 'to draw out' from the child. Engaging in the process of observing, Fröebel saw the teacher as an active participant in making meaning, not *for* the child, but *with* the child.

The following images show examples of the imaginative ways in which artist–educators encouraged children to explore their daily lives through art. Herr Josef Dworschak, a teacher in a Viennese orphanage in the 1930s, was concerned to develop children's imagination through a wide range of media such as painting, drawing, clay, woodwork, metal and glass. The painting on page 37 (below) is an example of how Dworschak inspired children to explore the use of colour on wet paper. This contrasted to the more usual practice in Viennese schools at the time of teaching about theories of colour. The examples of cursive writing patterns (page 38) are based on children's natural or 'free' movements. They show the flowing, rhythmic patterning that British artist–educator Marion Richardson sought to encourage in her position as District Art Inspector for the London County Council between 1930 and 1942. Frances Derham believed that fingerpainting — a technique developed by Ruth Faison Shaw in America in 1932 — was an important avenue of expression for a child, combining rhythmic movements, tactile connections and particular opportunities for children to experience colour mixing.

Observations of daily life

Through the use of different media and expressive techniques, artist–educators encouraged children towards a creative exploration of their daily lives. Children's art often depicts people in specific settings that enable the viewer to know something of their families and everyday activities. These Inuit children's paintings, for example, depict shared family and community activities — a mother prepares food as the children look on, children in hooded jackets play together with an animal. The richly detailed description of a celebration in South America shows the preparation of food, dancing, and eating. The food and implements on the table are carefully laid out and the painting captures precise details of furniture, costumes, and human gestures. Colour is used to emphasise contrasts, for example in the clothing details.

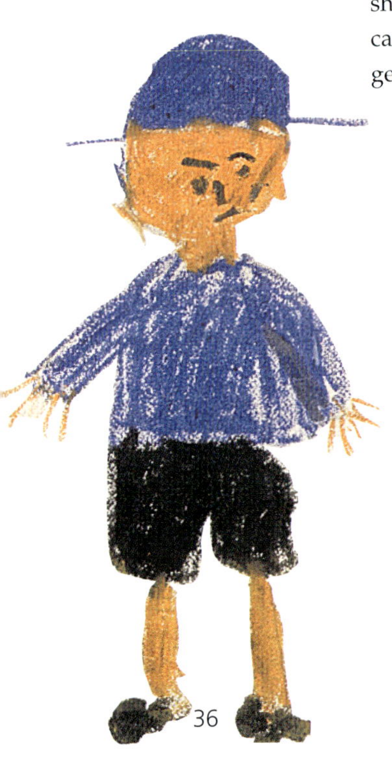

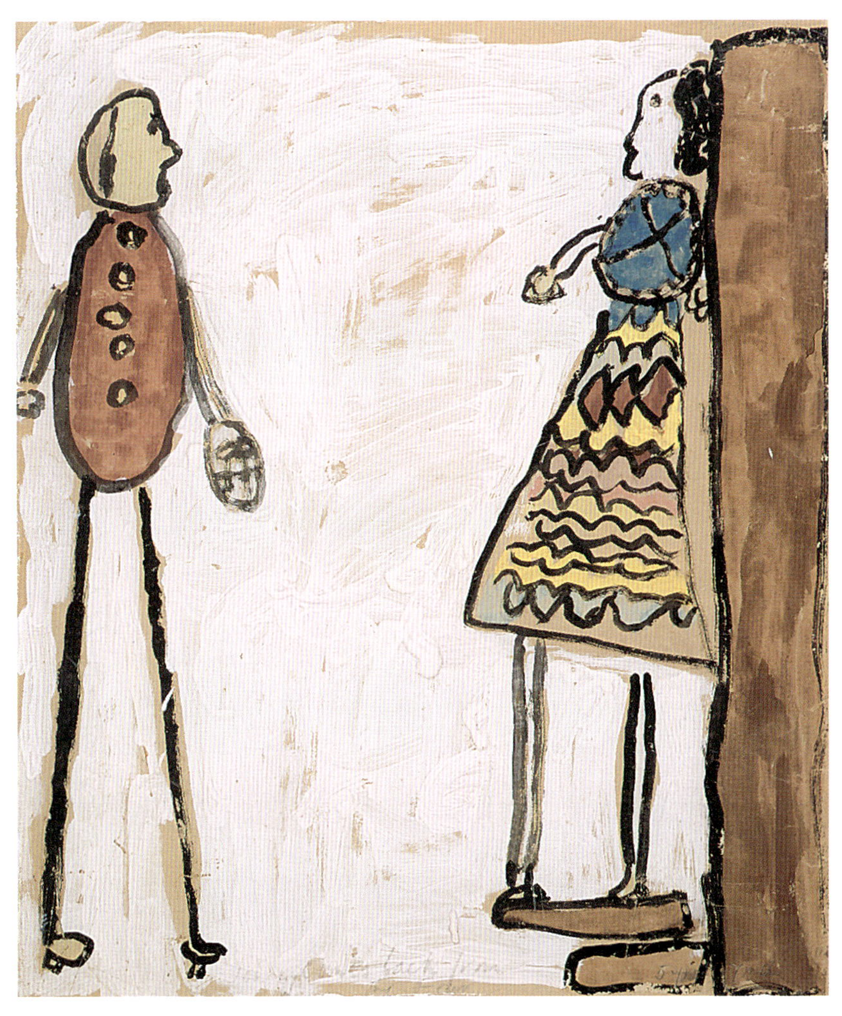

(left) **Unknown**
London
Johnny comes back from the fair
c.1930

(below) **Unknown**
Vienna
Animal, person, house c.1930

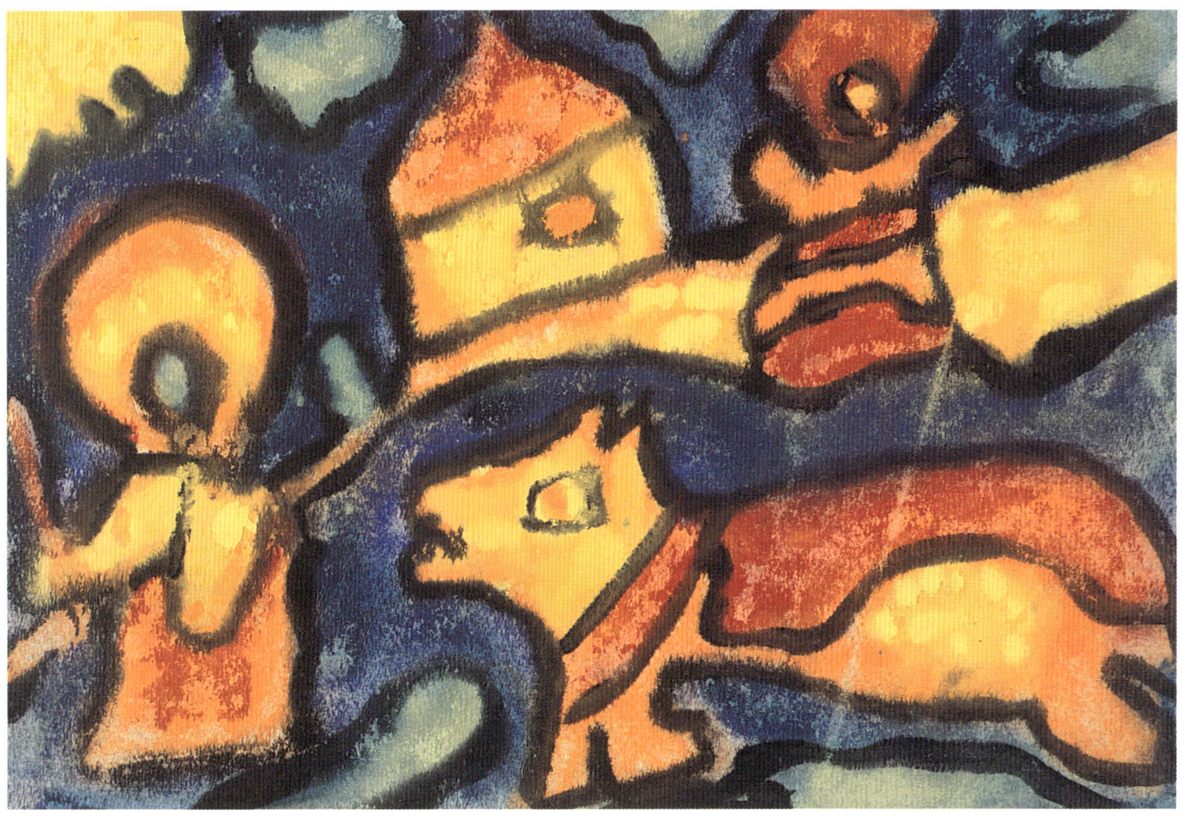

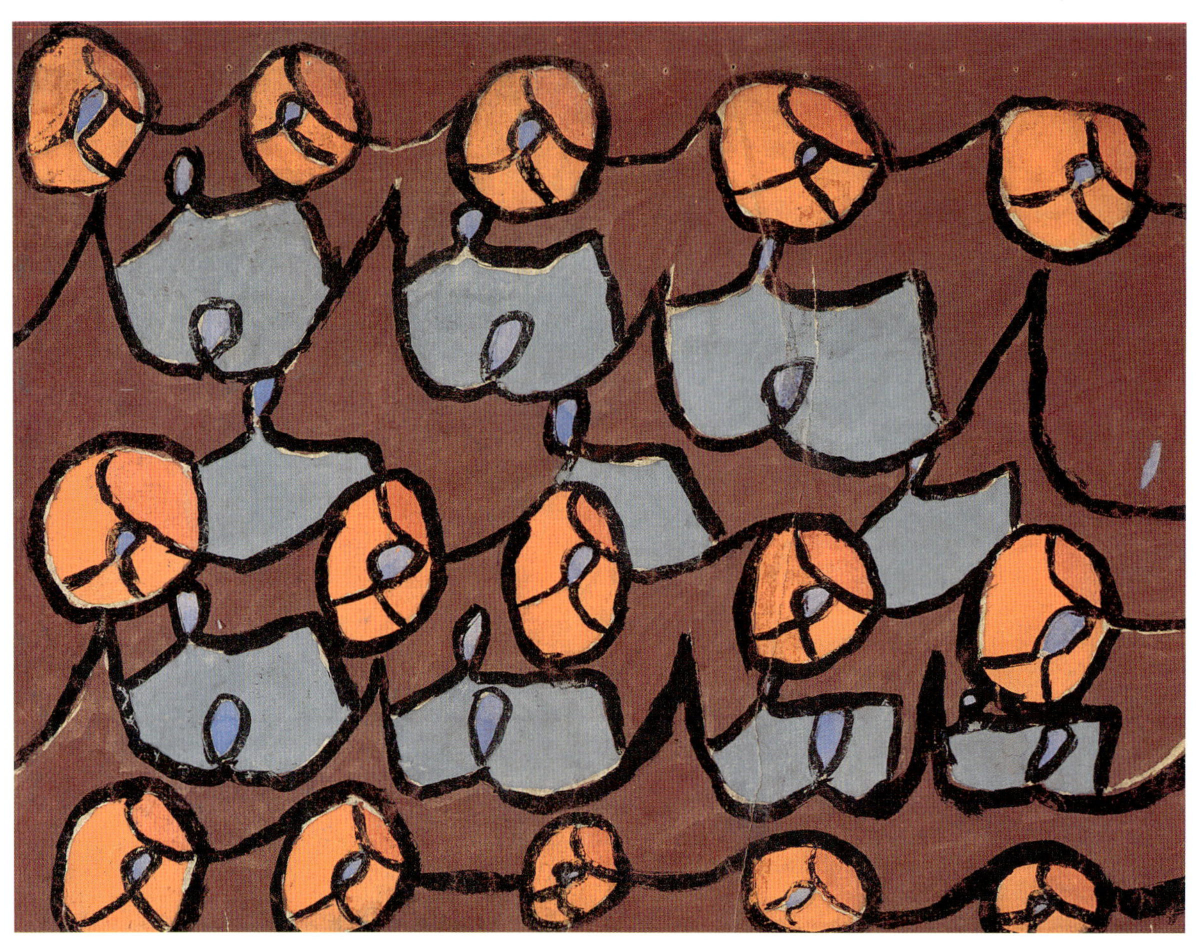

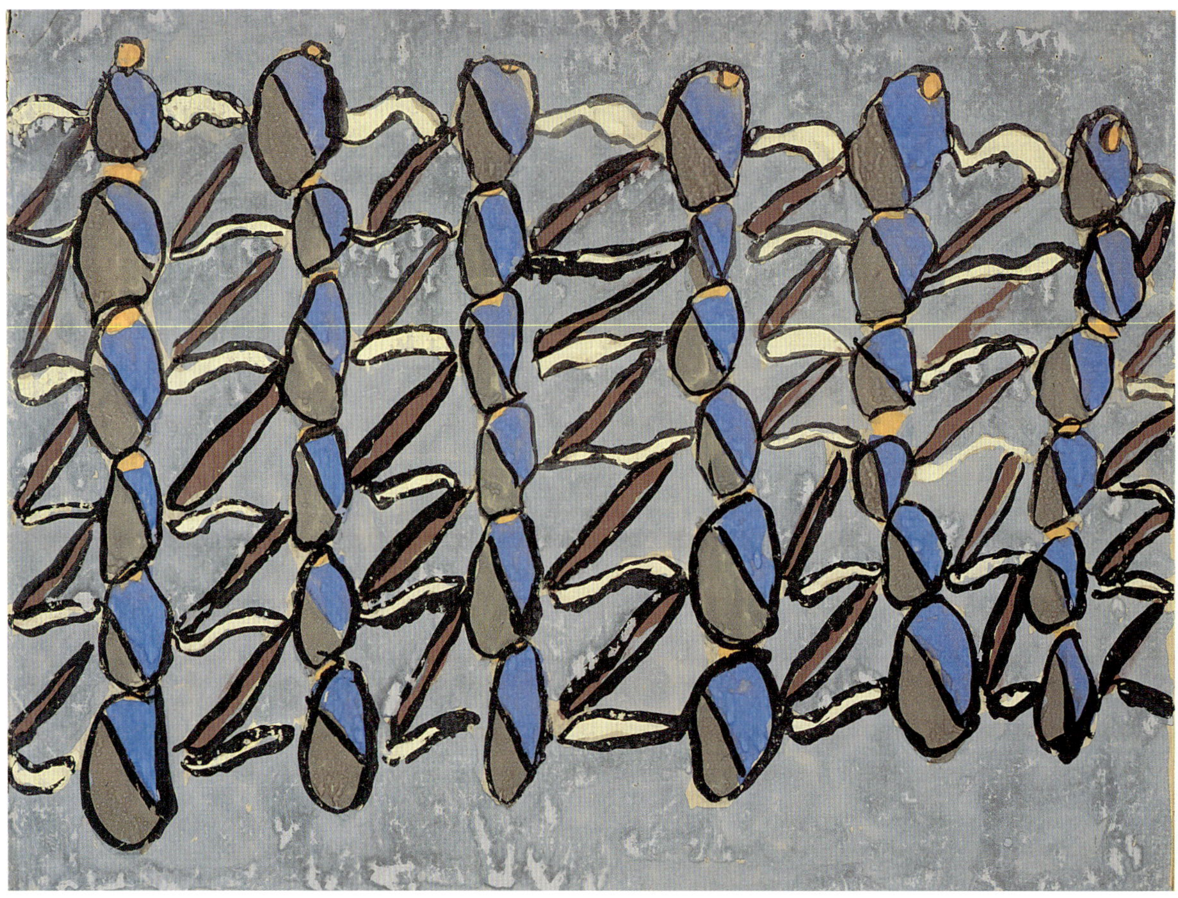

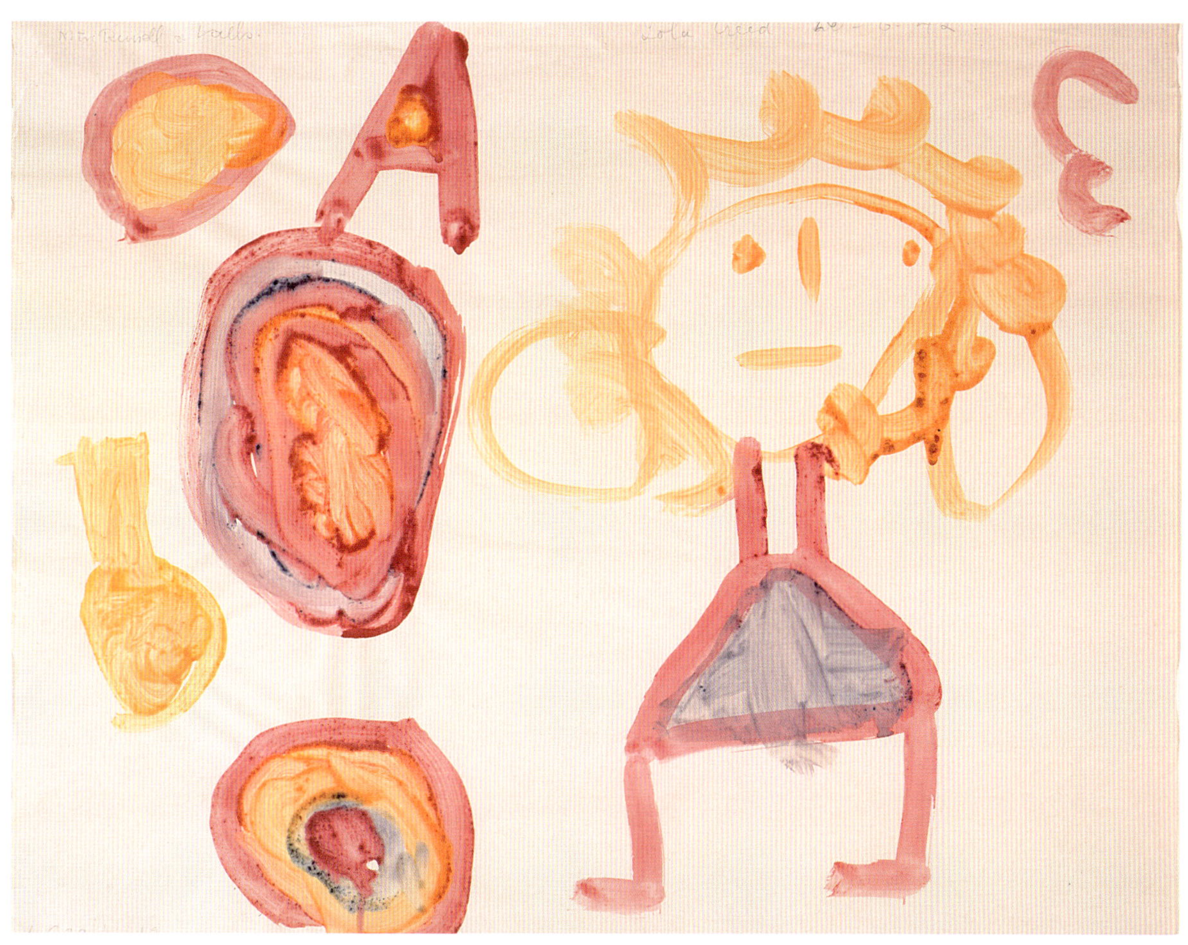

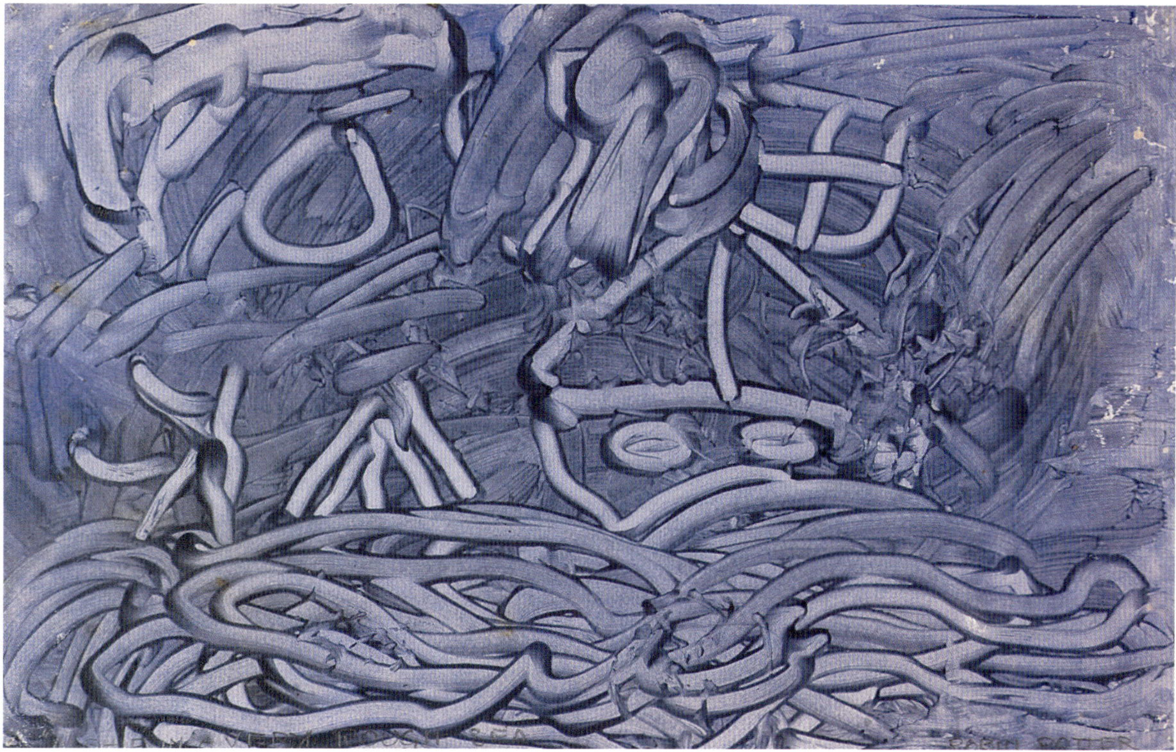

(above top) **Lola Creed** Australia, Melbourne *Miss Russell and balls* 1942
(above) **Robin Potter** Australia, Melbourne *A ship in a very rough sea* c.1940
(opposite above) **Joyce Cox** London *Writing pattern* c.1930
(opposite below) **Jessie Monk** London *Writing pattern* c.1930

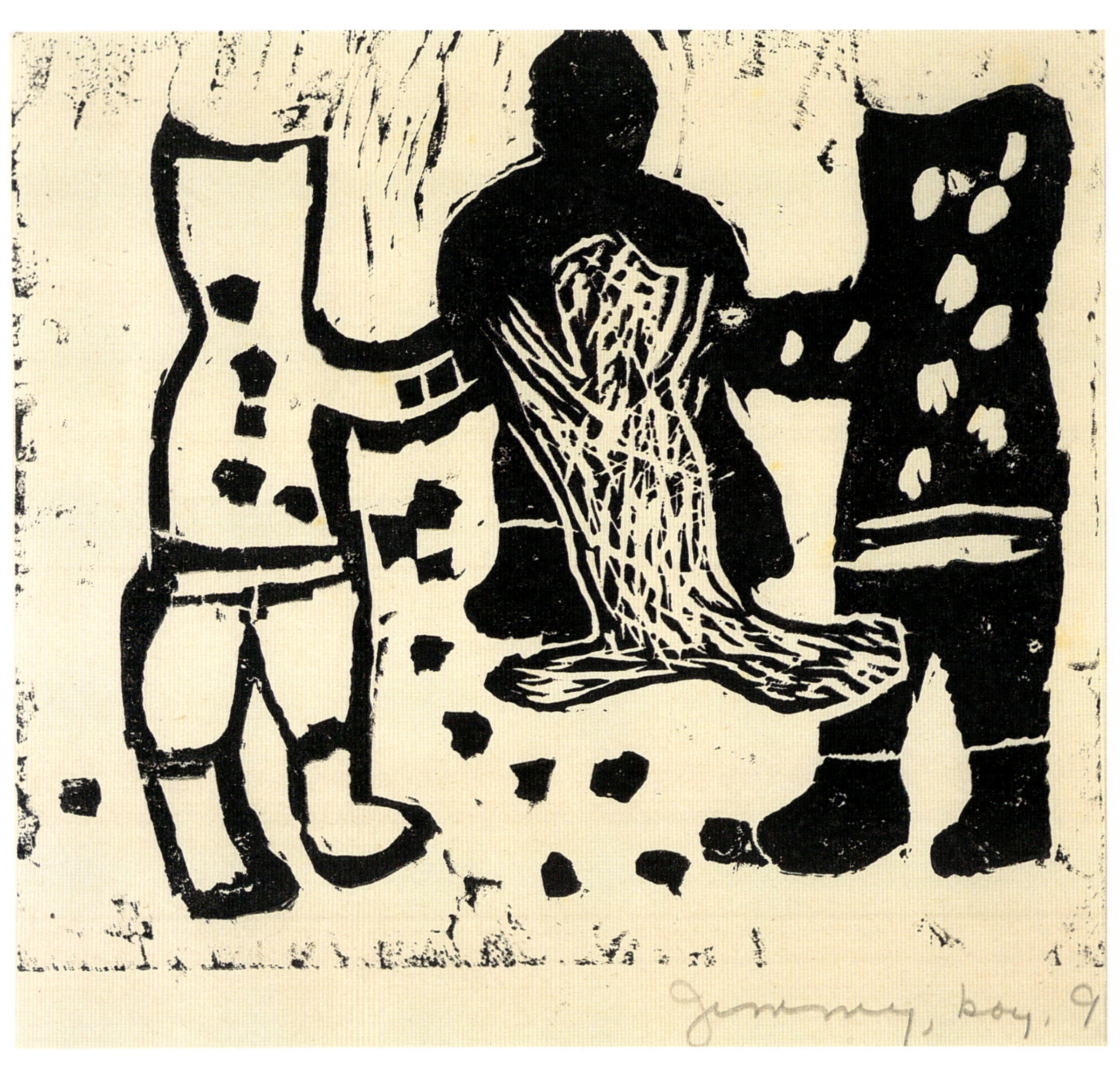

(above) **Jimmy** Canada Inuit *Children playing with an animal* c.1960
(opposite) **Itooloo** Canada Inuit *We watch mother clean the seal* c.1960

40

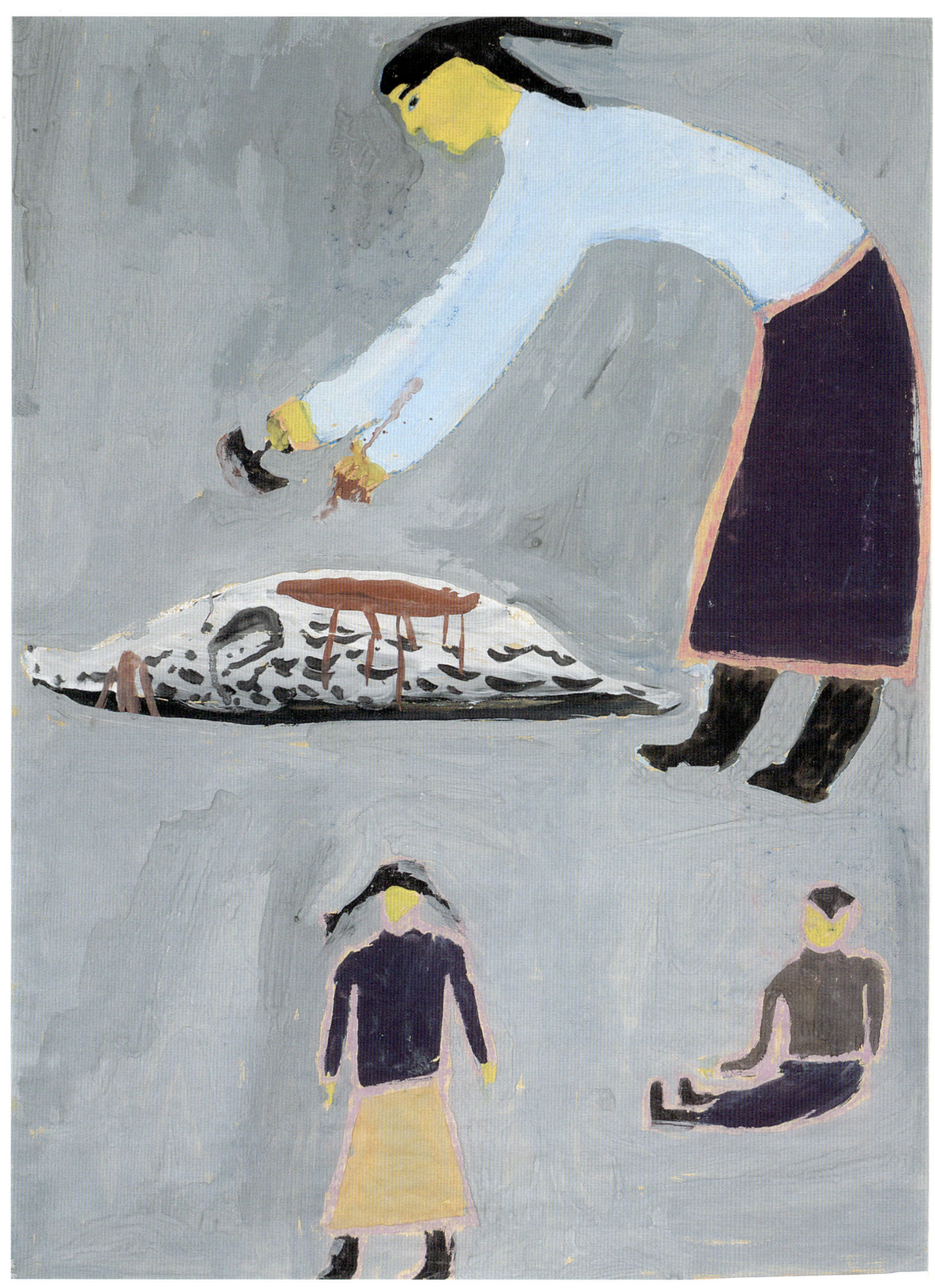

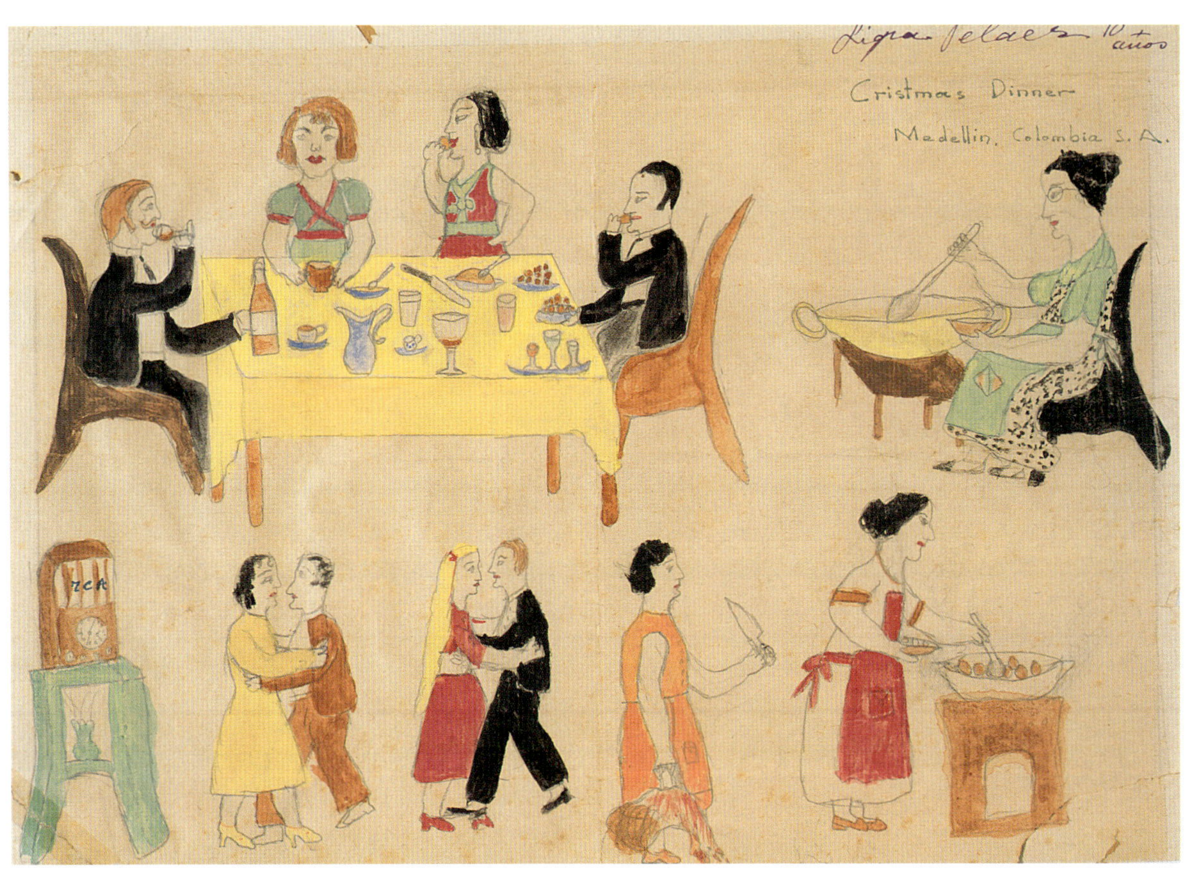

Cristmas Dinner
Madellin. Colombia S.A.

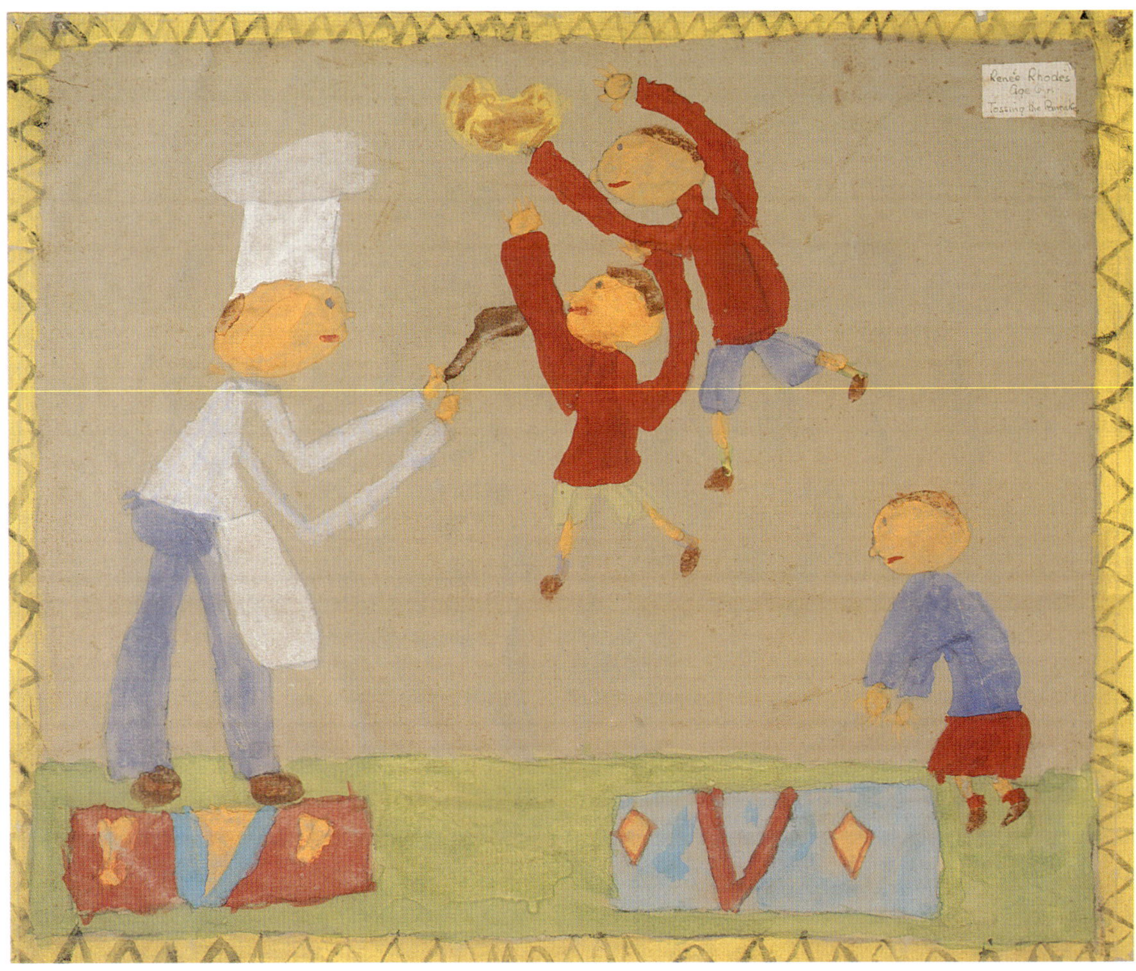

(right)
Hayashi
Japan
Man and a house c.1930

(below)
Elizabeth Pike
Australia, Melbourne
School's out c.1955

(opposite above)
Ligia Pelaes
South America
Christmas dinner c.1930

(opposite below)
Renee Rhodes
London
Tossing the pancake c.1930

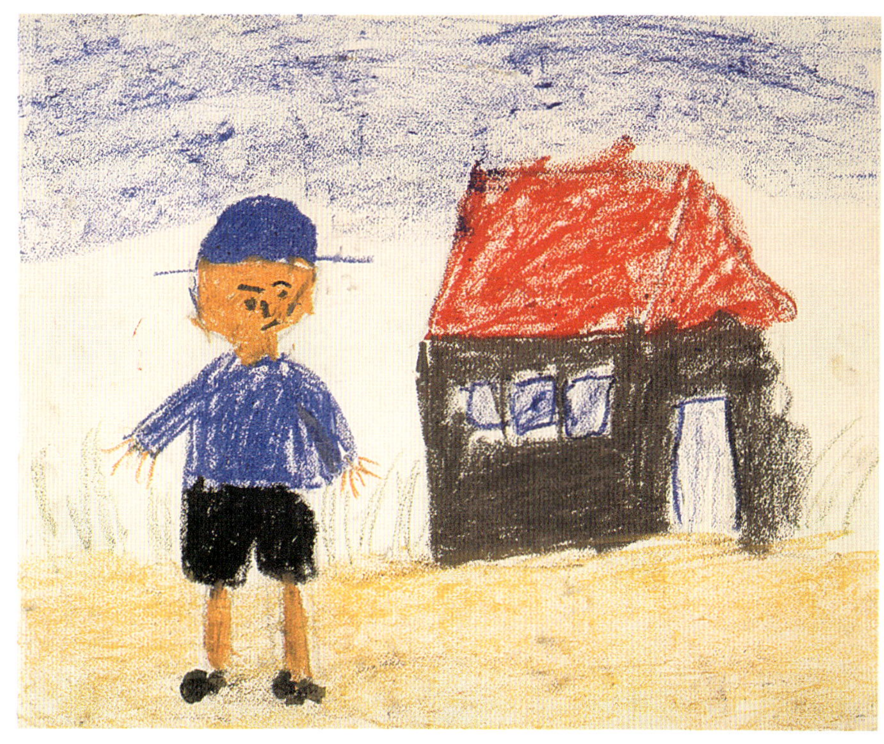

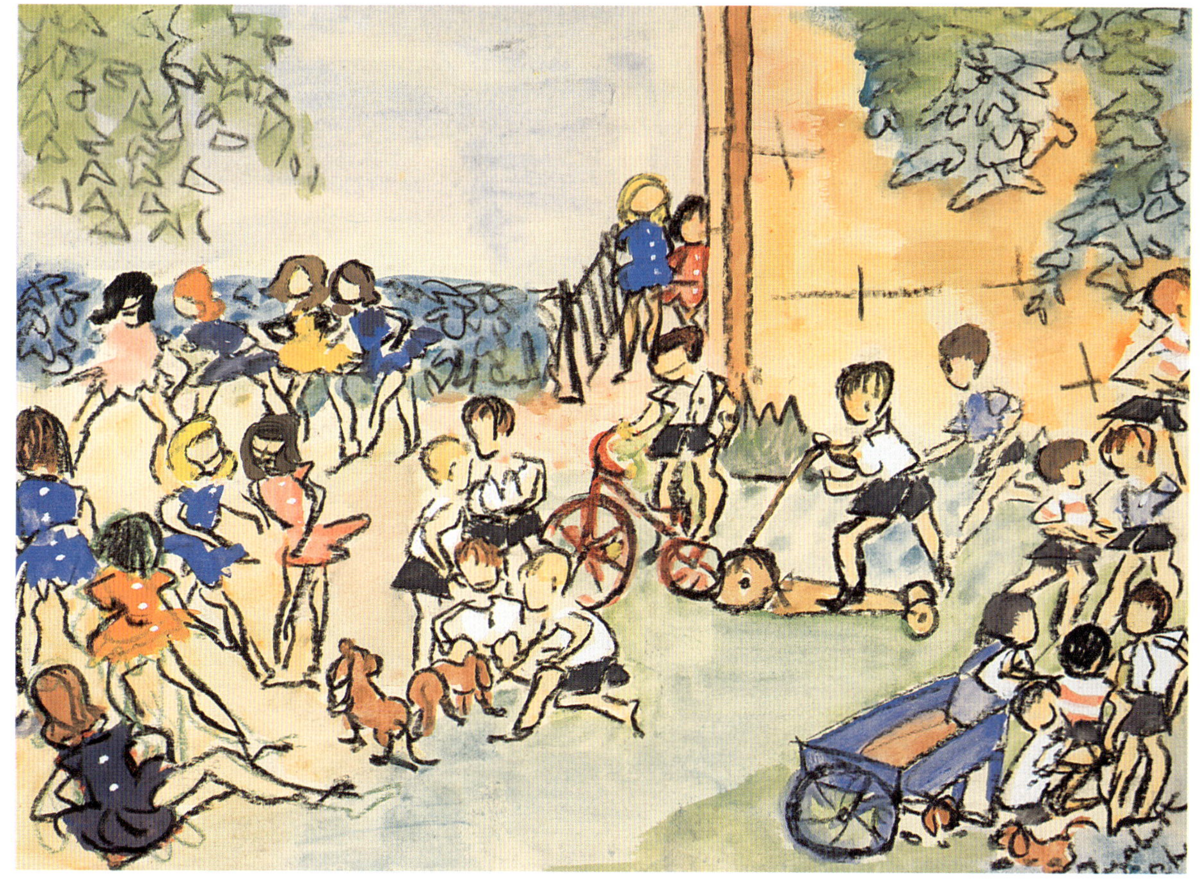

WORKS IN THE EXHIBITION

All works are in the Frances Derham Collection at the National Gallery of Australia, Canberra. The artist's place of residence and, where known, cultural background and age at the time the work was created are given after their name. Measurements are in centimetres, height before width.

SOCIAL AND POLITICAL EVENTS

Antony Baillieu
Australia, Melbourne 7yrs
Olympic swimming pool 1956
coloured pencil on paper
21.0 x 33.0cm
ELC43.307

Barrackina
Spain 12yrs
Helping the wounded c.1930
watercolour and pen on paper
20.2 x 27.6cm
ELC43.168

P. Baxter
Australia, Melbourne 7yrs
Come on Lorraine Crapp 1956
coloured pencil on paper
21.0 x 33.0cm
ELC43.268

K. Blasius
Austria
Nazi flags over Austria c.1930
watercolour on paper
22.0 x 27.8cm
ELC43.166

Rosa Candel
Spain 12yrs
Spanish village bombed c.1930
coloured pencil on paper
20.0 x 27.6cm
ELC43.163

Jamie Cumming
Australia, Melbourne
Someone climbing (She's going away) 1960
gouache on paper
61.0 x 43.6cm
ELC43.58

H. Dahrike
Austria
Raising the flag c.1930
watercolour on paper
25.0 x 34.0cm
ELC43.251

Garcia
Spain
Schoolroom c.1930
coloured pencil and pencil on paper
16.8 x 22.6cm
ELC43.190

Dormitory and schoolroom in an evacuation camp c.1930
coloured pencil and pencil on paper
17.4 x 22.6cm
ELC43.189

Grebenkin
Russia
A collective farm c.1930
watercolour and ink on paper
22.0 x 32.0cm
ELC43.181

C.E. Gustafsson
Finland
Depression 1934
gouache and pencil on paper
20.0 x 22.0cm
ELC43.49

Huguet
Spain
Destroyed home c.1930
coloured pencil and pen on paper
20.2 x 27.6cm
ELC43.169

Bombs over Barcelona c.1930
coloured pencil and pen on paper
20.2 x 27.6cm
ELC43.170

Kurochkin
Russia 13yrs
Demonstration c.1930
watercolour on paper
17.6 x 22.0cm
ELC43.182

T. Malo
Central America 10yrs
Building of the Panama Canal c.1930
pencil on paper
24.4 x 34.0cm
ELC43.50

Marian
Italy
Il Funerale de la Pinuccia c.1930
coloured pencil on paper
14.0 x 21.2cm
ELC43.46

di Mattia
Italy
Plane over church c.1930
coloured pencil on paper
14.0 x 14.0cm
ELC43.44

Popov
Russia 11yrs
Collective farm c.1930
watercolour and pencil on paper
14.8 x 21.0cm
ELC43.183

E. Puchol
Spain
Bombed building c.1930
coloured pencil and pen on paper
20.2 x 27.6cm
ELC43.167

Gheeli Sonnberg
Finland
Paper boy c.1930
material and newspaper on paper
24.2 x 19.4cm
ELC43.305

Ted
Australia, Melbourne, Lady Gowrie Child Centre
Ship 1942
paint and crayon on paper
45.8 x 58.4cm
ELC43.303

Uccio
Italy
Dropping bombs on a mountain village c.1930
coloured pencil and pencil on paper
12.2 x 17.0cm
ELC43.41

Unknown
Australia, Melbourne
Olympic torch 1956
coloured pencil on paper
18.6 x 27.4cm
ELC43.267

Voghera
Italy
Plane and soldiers c.1930
coloured pencil and pencil on paper
14.0 x 14.0cm
ELC43.40

PERSONAL AND CULTURAL IDENTITY

Joe Aguilar
United States of America, Navajo 12yrs
Three dancing figures with drum c.1930
gouache on paper
24.2 x 20.0cm
ELC43.171

Andrew B.
Papua New Guinea, Lahore, Port Moresby 4yrs
Hedgehog c.1960
dye and cornflour on paper
39.8 x 39.2cm
ELC43.255

Bessie
Australia, Hermannsburg
Palm Valley 1938
pencil on paper
38.0 x 25.2cm (folded)
ELC43.95

Rafael Brobla
Mexico 5yrs
Two boys
pencil and gouache on paper
38.6 x 29.6cm
ELC43.29

Collin
Australia, Hermannsburg
Landscape with rainbow snakes 1938
pastel on paper
25.4 x 37.4cm
ELC43.306

Davidee
Canada Inuit 13 yrs
Self portrait 1963
oil pastel on paper
30.2 x 23.0cm
ELC43.191

June Enock
Papua New Guinea 14yrs
Malabunga, East New Britain
Untitled *c.*1967
paint on paper
44.4 x 57.4cm
ELC43.221

A. Glover
Australia, Sydney 13yrs
*Circular Quay c.*1940
gouache on paper
40.4 x 56.0cm
ELC43.246

Jose S. Herrera
United States of America, New Mexico
Navajo 11yrs
*Two dancing figures c.*1930
gouache on paper
20.0 x 24.8cm
ELC43.179

*Harvesting corn c.*1930
gouache on paper
21.6 x 29.2cm
ELC43.172

Immanuel
Australia, Hermannsburg
Homestead 1938
coloured pencil and pastel on paper
19.4 x 56.0cm
ELC43.215

Sailor Koomdtta
Australia, Aurukun 12yrs
Untitled 1948
oil pastel and pencil on paper
21.0 x 16.4cm
ELC43.259

Bobbie Kummara
Australia, Aurukun 11yrs
Stockmen mustering the cow 1948
oil pastel and pencil on paper
16.6 x 21.0cm
ELC43.260

Tonita Lujan
United States of America, Navajo
*Taos women baking bread c.*1930
gouache on paper
25.4 x 35.8cm
ELC43.66

Massey
Australia, Hermannsburg
Landscape — Palm Valley 1938
pastel and pencil on paper
14.0 x 20.0cm
ELC43.133

A. Monies
Papua New Guinea
*Three headed monster c.*1967
oil pastel on paper
38.2 x 56.0cm
ELC43.220

Boongie Nindarngar
Australia, Western Australia,
Mt Margaret Mission 13yrs
Mission map 1939
coloured pencil, ink and pencil
on paper
27.8 x 38.0cm
ELC43.277

NK
Australia, Aurukun
Four barramundi 1948
watercolour on paper
36.2 x 45.8cm
ELC43.273

Arthur Pambegan
Australia, Aurukun 11yrs
Outdoor scene with kangaroo hunt 1948
coloured pencil and pencil on paper
16.2 x 21.0cm
ELC43.261

Maud Pamkotchata
Australia, Aurukun
Mrs Derham on the water tank 1948
oil pastel and pencil on paper
16.6 x 20.2cm
ELC43.263

Brian Pamtoonda
Australia, Aurukun 12–13yrs
Pig hunting 1948
oil pastel and pencil on paper
17.0 x 21.0cm
ELC43.258

Claude Panka
Australia, Hermannsburg
Aeroplane 1938
pastel on paper
29.6 x 49.6cm
ELC43.99

Horse and rider 1938
pastel on paper
31.0 x 41.2cm
ELC43.245

Aeroplane with map of Australia 1938
pastel on paper
29.4 x 49.6cm
ELC43.101

Percy
Australia, Hermannsburg
The church 1938
dye and starch on paper
33.0 x 48.0cm
ELC43.107

Quevedo
South America 12yrs
*Grain sellers c.*1930
gouache and pencil on paper
10.4 x 22.0cm
ELC43.25

Sarah
Canada Inuit
Self-portrait 1963
oil pastel on paper
30.2 x 23.0cm
ELC43.192

Unknown
United States of America, Navajo
*Two feathered dancers and a drummer
c.*1930
gouache on paper
19.8 x 27.4cm
ELC43.178

Unknown
South America
*Pottery sellers c.*1930
gouache and pencil on paper
10.4 x 22.0cm
ELC43.26

Unknown
South America
*Musicians c.*1930
gouache and pencil on paper
10.4 x 22.0cm
ELC43.27

Unknown
South America
*Kitchenware c.*1930
gouache and pencil on paper
10.4 x 22.0cm
ELC43.28

Unknown
Australia, Hermannsburg
Hermannsburg Mission 1938
pastel and pencil on paper
15.2 x 43.8cm
ELC43.212

Unknown
Australia, Aurukun
*Pig c.*1948
dye and cornflour on paper
27.0 x 37.4cm
ELC43.5

Unknown
Papua New Guinea 10–15yrs
*Legendary figures with snake and fire
c.*1960
oil pastel and paint on paper
38.2 x 56.0cm
ELC43.175

Unknown
Papua New Guinea 10–15yrs
*Cannibals c.*1967
oil pastel on paper
38.2 x 56.0cm
ELC43.180

Takeshi Yamazaki
Japan
*Woman in green hat c.*1930
gouache and ink on paper
27.2 x 24.2cm
ELC43.69

SCHOOL AND FAMILY LIFE

Joyce Cox
London
*Writing pattern c.*1930
crayon and gouache on paper
38.4 x 50.6cm
ELC43.91

Lola Creed
Australia, Melbourne
Miss Russell and balls 1942
dye and cornflour on paper
45.8 x 58.4cm
ELC43.22

Juan Gisalt
Mexcio
Woman in apron c.1930
pencil and gouache on paper
35.0 x 25.0cm
ELC43.34

Hayashi
Japan 6yrs
Man and a house c.1930
oil pastel on paper
40.8 x 50.8cm
ELC43.247

Itooloo
Canada Inuit 14yrs
We watch mother clean the seal c.1960
tempera on paper
71.6 x 53.6cm
ELC43.173

Jimmy
Canada Inuit 9yrs
Children playing with an animal c.1960
linocut, ink on paper
17.2 x 20.4cm
ELC43.187

This is Cape Dorset 1960
linocut, ink on paper
15.4 x 30.6cm
ELC43.188

Kauper
Vienna
Figure in light c.1930
gouache on paper
29.6 x 19.8cm
ELC43.231

Jessie Monk
London
Writing pattern c.1930
crayon and gouache on paper
38.0 x 50.8cm
ELC43.88

Ligia Pelaes
South America
Christmas dinner c.1930
gouache and pencil on paper
24.8 x 34.8cm
ELC43.47

Elizabeth Pike
Australia, Melbourne
School's out c.1955
gouache and crayon on paper
30.6 x 37.8cm
ELC43.111

Robin Potter
Australia, Melbourne
A ship in a very rough sea c.1940
dye and cornflour on paper
30.2 x 48.6cm
ELC43.12

Dimity Reed
Australia, Melbourne
Reach for the apple 1951
pastel and pencil on paper
38.6 x 38.6cm
ELC43.302

Renee Rhodes
London
Tossing the pancake c.1930
watercolour on paper
51.0 x 61.2cm
ELC43.57

Ernestina Turrel
Mexico
Portrait (Girl skipping) c.1930
gouache and pencil on paper
38.8 x 23.2cm
ELC43.35

Unknown
London
Johnny comes back from the fair c.1930
dye and starch on paper
58.8 x 50.8cm
ELC43.87

Unknown
Vienna
Houses c.1930
gouache on paper
24.2 x 31.2cm
ELC43.229

Unknown
Vienna
Animal, person, house c.1930
gouache on paper
29.8 x 29.6cm
ELC43.230

Unknown
Vienna
Baby c.1930
gouache on paper
15.2 x 22.6cm
ELC43.238

Eve Wordsworth
Australia, Melbourne 8yrs
Reach for the apple 1968
charcoal on paper
38.0 x 27.6cm
ELC43.151

WORKS BY FRANCES DERHAM

(Due to the fragile nature of these
works, the selection shown will vary
according to venue)

Frances DERHAM
Australia 1894–1987
Moonlight 1911
Melbourne
stencil, printed in colour on card
6.5 x 6.5cm
1987.431

Happy holidays (1920–21)
Melbourne
stencil, printed in colour on paper
6.2 x 8.2cm
1982.1753

*Greeting card: Christmas Dr and Mrs
Alfred Derham* (1924)
Melbourne
linocut, printed in colour on paper
6.0 x 12.6cm
1982.1755

Sydney bridge 1929
Melbourne
linocut, printed in colour on paper
17.8 x 25.9cm
1980.2230

Aboriginal hunter 1930
Melbourne
linocut, printed in brown ink on paper
8.3 x 19.0cm
82.1756

Piece of fabric; koala and possum motifs
1931
Melbourne
potato cut on linen
51.0 x 33.0cm
1981.322

Tom, David and Bill at the seaside
(c.1932–3)
Melbourne
linocut, printed in colour on paper
11.4 x 14.0cm
82.1762

Greeting card: Christmas 1934
Melbourne
linocut on paper
4.6 x 7.4cm
Gift of James Mollison 1984
84.291

Kangaroo (1934)
Melbourne
linocut on paper
4.6 x 7.4cm
1982.1764

Aboriginal artists (1936)
Melbourne
linocut, printed in colour on paper
11.8 x 11.8cm
1982.1766

*Cover design for pamphlet for the Nursery
Kindergarten Extension Board* 1942
Melbourne
linocut on paper
21.0 x 14.5cm
1982.1768

Sheet of various images; flowers, animals
(1943)
Melbourne
linocut on card
22.4 x 31.9cm
1982.1769

FURTHER READING

Selected references by Frances Derham

Derham, Frances, 'Seeking Child Art in "The Centre" ', *The Argus Weekend Magazine*, October 22, 1938, p.3.

Derham, Frances, *Art for Little Children*, Perth: University of Western Australia, Adult Education Board Box Scheme, E284, 1939.

Derham, Frances, 'The Art of Children', *Australian Artist*, vol. 1, no. 2, 1947, pp.46–8.

Derham, Frances, *Art for the Child Under Seven*, Canberra: Australian Preschool Association, 1961. (Further editions: second, 1962; third, 1967; fourth, 1970; fifth, 1973.)

Selected references about art, child art and Derham

Cumpston, J.H.L. & Heinig, C., *Preschool Centres in Australia: Building, equipment and programme*, Canberra: Commonwealth of Australia, Department of Health, 1944.

Hardy, Jane, 'Visitors to Hermannsburg: An essay on cross cultural learning', in Hardy, Jane, Megaw, J.S.V. & Megaw, Ruth M. (eds), *The Heritage of Namatjira: The watercolourists of Central Australia*, Port Melbourne: William Heinemann, 1992.

Hoff, Jennifer, *Drawings and Paintings by Children from Hermannsburg, Aurukun and Malabunga*, Canberra: Australian National Gallery, 1984.

Isaacs, Jennifer, *The Gentle Arts: 200 years of women's domestic and decorative arts*, Willoughby, NSW: Ure Smith Press, 1987.

Lowenfeld, Viktor, *The Nature of Creative Activity*, London: Routledge and Kegan Paul, 1939.

Mountford, Charles Percy, *The Art of Albert Namatjira*, Melbourne: Bread and Cheese Club, 1944.

Piscitelli, Barbara, 'Frances Derham and the Expressive Arts: Her life and legacy', *Australian Journal of Early Childhood*, vol. 18, no. 1, 1993, pp.4–10.

Piscitelli, Barbara, The Life of Frances Derham: Process, product and reflections, unpublished PhD dissertation, James Cook University of North Queensland, Townsville, 1994.

Richardson, Marion, *Art and the Child*, London: University of London Press, 1948.

Smith, Bernard (ed.), *Education through Art in Australia*, Melbourne: Melbourne University Press, 1958.

Stevenson, C. & White, M., 'Children's Art Exhibitions: The contexts and challenges', *Children's Environments*, vol. 12, no. 3, 1995.

White M. & Stevenson, C., *Drawing on the Art of Children: An historical perspective of children's art in the twentieth century*, Sydney: Macquarie University, 1997.

Wilson, Francesca, *The Child as Artist: Some Conversations with Professor Cizek*, London: Children's Art Exhibition Fund, 1921.

ABOUT THE AUTHORS

Dr Barbara Piscitelli is Senior Lecturer and Principal Researcher in the Faculty of Education at Queensland University of Technology. Over the past decade Dr Piscitelli has studied historical, contemporary and cross-cultural influences on children's art education. She has created a number of exhibitions of children's art, including *Children's Global Vision: A world of art* (1999), *Children Have Rights* (1997), *Together Under One Sun* (1995) and *Our World* (1993).

Margaret White lectures at Macquarie University in arts, creativity and history. Her present research into cultures of childhood in the twentieth century is linked with the curating of exhibitions, the development of arts projects for children and adults, and the shaping of new perspectives on teaching, learning and the arts. Her earlier work with children included a period at Preshil in Melbourne.

Ron Ramsey has worked with the National Gallery of Australia since 1991. He was manager of the Travelling Exhibitions Program from 1991 to 1995 and Head of Education and Public Programs from 1995 to 1999. As General Manager, Access and Education, Mr Ramsey now manages the Gallery's exhibitions program and public access activities.